DATE DUE		
NOV 17 2006		
JUL 17 2007		

The Accidental System

Dilemmas in American Politics

Series Editor   L. Sandy Maisel, *Colby College*

Dilemmas in American Politics offers teachers and students a series of quality books on timely topics and key institutions in American government. Each text will examine a "real world" dilemma and will be structured to cover the historical, theoretical, policy relevant, and future dimensions of its subject.

••

BOOKS IN THIS SERIES

• •

The Accidental System: Health Care Policy in America, Michael D. Reagan

The Image-Is-Everything Presidency: Dilemmas of American Leadership, Richard W. Waterman, Robert Wright, and Gilbert St. Clair

"Can We All Get Along?" Racial and Ethnic Minorities in American Politics, Second Edition, Updated, Paula D. McClain and Joseph Stewart Jr.

The Dysfunctional Congress? The Individual Roots of an Institutional Dilemma, Kenneth R. Mayer and David T. Canon

Checks & Balances? How a Parliamentary System Could Change American Politics, Paul Christopher Manuel and Anne Marie Cammisa

Remote and Controlled: Media Politics in a Cynical Age, Second Edition, Matthew Robert Kerbel

The Angry American: How Voter Rage Is Changing the Nation, Second Edition, Susan J. Tolchin

Two Parties—Or More? The American Party System, John F. Bibby and L. Sandy Maisel

Making Americans, Remaking America: Immigration and Immigrant Policy, Louis DeSipio and Rodolfo O. de la Garza

From Rhetoric to Reform? Welfare Policy in American Politics, Anne Marie Cammisa

The New Citizenship: Unconventional Politics, Activism, and Service, Craig A. Rimmerman

No Neutral Ground? Abortion Politics in an Age of Absolutes, Karen O'Connor

Onward Christian Soldiers? The Religious Right in American Politics, Clyde Wilcox

Payment Due: A Nation in Debt, A Generation in Trouble, Timothy J. Penny and Steven E. Schier

Bucking the Deficit: Economic Policymaking in the United States, G. Calvin Mackenzie and Saranna Thornton

The
Accidental
System

....

Health Care Policy
in America

Michael D. Reagan
University of California, Riverside

Westview Press
A Member of the Perseus Books Group

Dilemmas in American Politics

Copyright © 1999 by Westview Press, A Member of the Perseus Books Group

Published in 1999 in the United States of America by Westview Press, 5500 Central Avenue, Boulder, Colorado 80301-2877, and in the United Kingdom by Westview Press, 12 Hid's Copse Road, Cumnor Hill, Oxford OX2 9JJ

Library of Congress Cataloging-in-Publication Data
Reagan, Michael D.
    The accidental system : health care policy in America / Michael D. Reagan.
        p.   cm. — (Dilemmas in American politics)
    Includes bibliographical references and index.
    ISBN 0-8133-9997-1 (hc). — ISBN 0-8133-9996-3 (pbk.)
    1. Medical policy—United States.   2. Medical care—United States.
I. Title.   II. Series.
RA395.A3R36   1999
362.1'0973—dc21   98-55763
                                                                                              CIP

The paper used in this publication meets the requirements of the American National Standard for Permanence of Paper for Printed Library Materials Z39.48-1984.

10   9   8   7   6   5   4   3   2   1

Contents

Tables and Photos

Tables

Photos

Acronyms

AAHP	American Association of Health Plans
AARP	American Association of Retired Persons
AFDC	Aid to Families with Dependent Children
AHCPR	Agency for Health Care Policy and Research
AMA	American Medical Association
AMPAC	American Medical Political Action Committee
BBA	Balanced Budget Act of 1997
BOB	Bureau of the Budget
CBO	Congressional Budget Office
CDC	Centers for Disease Control
CMA	Canadian Medical Association
CPI	Consumer Price Index
DHHS	Department of Health and Human Services
DRG	diagnostic related group
EPO	exclusive provider organization
ER	emergency room
ERISA	Employee Retirement Income Security Act
ESRD	end-stage renal disease
FACCT	Foundation for Accountability
FDA	Food and Drug Administration
FFS	fee-for-service
GAO	General Accounting Office
GDP	gross domestic product
HCFA	Health Care Financing Administration
HEDIS	Health Plan Employer Data and Information Set
HIAA	Health Insurance Association of America
HMO	health maintenance organization
IPA	independent practice association
JCAHCO	Joint Commission on Accreditation of Health Care Organizations
LC	lowest cost
LTC	long-term care
M&M	Medicare and Medicaid

MA	maximum access
MedPAC	Medicare Payment Advisory Commission
MQ	maximum quality
MSA	medical savings account
MSO	management service organization
NAACP	National Association for the Advancement of Colored People
NCHS	National Center for Health Statistics
NCQA	National Committee for Quality Assurance
NFIB	National Federation of Independent Business
NGA	National Governors Association
NHS	National Health Service
NIH	National Institutes of Health
OMB	Office of Management and Budget
OOP	out-of-pocket
OR	operating room
PAC	political action committee
POS	point of service
PPO	preferred provider organization
PPRC	Physician Payment Review Commission
PPS	Prospective Payment System
ProPAC	Prospective Payment Assessment Commission
PSO	provider service organization
PSO	provider sponsored organization
RBRVS	resource-based relative value scale
RSG	Reforming States Group
RVS	relative value scale
SNF	skilled nursing facility
TANF	Temporary Assistance to Needy Families
UHI	universal health insurance
UR	utilization review
VA	Veterans Affairs
VPS	volume performance standard

The Accidental System

1

The Basic Dilemma

*Is Health Care a Right or a
Market Commodity?*

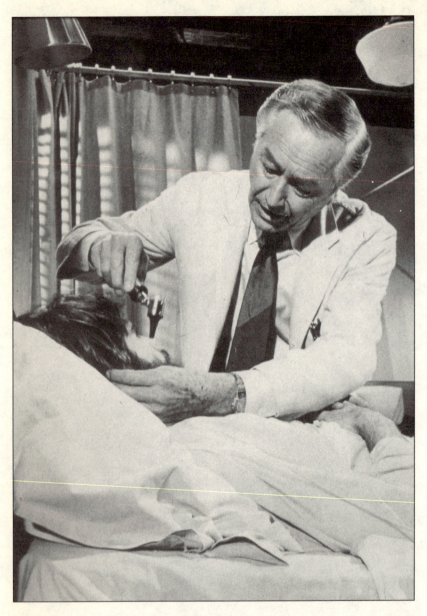

Robert Young, portraying Marcus Welby, examines a patient in a scene from *Marcus Welby, MD*. Photo courtesy of Archive Photos, reprinted with permission.

Aᴍᴇʀɪᴄᴀɴ ᴍᴇᴅɪᴄᴀʟ ᴄᴀʀᴇ ɪs often asserted to be the "best in the world." It is certainly the most high tech and can with few exceptions provide more complex, sophisticated treatments than can doctors and hospitals in any other country. In that sense, the "best" claim is supportable. Yet when one considers that 43.4 million Americans lack health insurance[1] despite per capita health care expenditures nearly double those of most other industrial countries, the claim rings hollow for many. Best for whom? is their question.

Lack of medical insurance coverage is the most widespread "disease" in the United States, one whose origin lies in the inadequacy of the private health care marketplace—in particular Americans' primary reliance on the decisions of private employers to offer, or not, group coverage for their workers. The practice of medicine at the level of the physician or the nurse is a profession, but health care is an industry whose economic characteristics vitally affect the practice of its professions. The coverage shortfall reflects the U.S. refusal to recognize the contradiction implicit in two widely held assertions:

- Everyone should have the best of whatever health care is needed, *but*
- government should keep out of it and market choices (mostly by employers) should determine the availability of coverage.

There, in a nutshell, is the dilemma: how to assure that necessary care is received while treating medical care as one more private good to be bought and sold like cars, or furniture, or financial services—with the difference that those products and services are usually sold on an individual basis, whereas the great bulk of health insurance is purchased by employers to cover a group of employees. To understand the nature of American health care therefore requires that we take a side trip into the basic language of economics. In the simple institutional sense that the vast bulk of property, personal and business, has been privately held, the United States has always been a capitalist country. In the ideological sense, preindustrial mercantilist ideas (which saw a substantial role for government in guiding the development of economic infrastructure) remained influential before the Civil War. Laissez-faire ideology (roughly, keep

government out of the way) came to the fore as late nineteenth-century indus-
trialism developed. In substantial degree it has remained the dominant economic creed ever since, with major exceptions in the Progressive and New Deal
periods. The United States does have some publicly (i.e., governmentally)
owned enterprises; for example, the Postal Service, national laboratories in the
nuclear industry, and the Tennessee Valley Authority. Even some hospitals are
government owned—at the national level, hospitals for veterans, and at the local level, county-owned general hospitals serving mostly the poor. But government enterprises are few in number, and each has had a unique rationale.

Unlike most other industrial nations, the United States has never been satisfied simply to *be* capitalist. Americans have insisted that "free enterprise" is
"the American way." And the phrase "democratic capitalism" is used as a sort of
mantra in after-dinner speeches. Although much reasoned argument and
some evidence support the notion that economic and political freedoms frequently go together, some clearly healthy democracies (e.g., the Scandinavian
countries) have far higher shares of their economic activity in the public sector
than does the United States. Democratic capitalism is a warm and fuzzy
phrase, not an empirically based concept. For example, are corporations democratic organizations because stockholders vote on the board of directors?
Not exactly: Instead of one person–one vote, it's one share–one vote. In the
public elections sphere the United States abandoned a property qualification
for voting back in the 1840s. In other words, free enterprise is more an ideological theme than a fact. Nowhere is the gap between reality and Americans'
rhetorical enthusiasms greater—and more dangerously misleading—than in
the health care industry. And what an industry it is, accounting for 1 trillion
dollars a year, one-seventh of the entire economy.[2]

Although nearly half of health care is financed publicly (including
Medicare, Medicaid, armed forces and veterans health care, public health offices, the National Institutes of Health, and the Centers for Disease Control, to
mention just a few), the battle cry of the day is that the system can be fixed if
only Americans prescribe larger doses of a nostrum called market competition. It is indeed clear that health care competition increased as the number of
health maintenance organizations (HMOs) and similar managed care organizations multiplied over more than two decades. There are, however, some
problems.

Some health economists who favor a market competition approach have acknowledged that some government regulatory provisions are needed to set
boundaries on the competition. Industry spokespersons, however, generally ignore that advice, despite the fact that economic competition without some

kind of publicly set framework of law would be warfare, not competition. It was, after all, Adam Smith rather than Karl Marx who wrote of a need for regulation of business to protect the consuming public. The more noticeable problem from a newspaper reader's perspective is that private HMO competition has taken forms that help firms make money by avoiding patients likely to get sick and by making it difficult to get a doctor's appointment when the problem is routine rather than urgent. Competition is being used less to bring health care to the average person at the lowest possible cost than as a way of controlling costs paid by employers and governments. Cost control of this kind sometimes means passing on more costs to individual employees, with more of them then deciding to forego coverage. Sometimes managed care organizations or individual providers pursuing cost control have accepted low reimbursement rates to gain patients and then have found that they have too little income to provide high-quality care.

Patient dissatisfaction is strong, as evidenced by the rush of legislators to appease voter-patients with legislation that micromanages health care delivery—even though very few lawmakers have medical credentials. To demonstrate Americans' inconsistency regarding government's role in the economy, note that public demand for regulation of inpatient stays for birthing and mastectomies followed within two years the vehement public rejection of President Clinton's 1994 health care reform bill. The bill was rejected on the ground that Americans should "keep government out of health care," as television commercials sponsored by the Health Insurance Association of America effectively argued.

In short, as a voting public Americans tend toward schizophrenia in their views about private and public roles in health care—with one crucial exception: They clearly believe that every American should receive all the medical care she or he needs. Asked if it was a proper role of government to make sure everyone has access to quality medical care regardless of his or her ability to pay, 84 percent of respondents said "yes" in a late 1996 poll.

What's Wrong with the Market Model?

Why do the concept of a right to health care and Americans' ideological bent toward private enterprise conflict with one another? The answer lies in comparing the qualities of a true textbook marketplace with the characteristics of health care as a private "product." What economists have long termed "perfect competition" is a model with some specific requirements:

- The consumer decides autonomously what product or service she wishes to buy.
- The product must be interchangeable from one supply to another—such as bushels of wheat—and there must be easy entry of new competitors.
- There are many suppliers—too many for any one to monopolize price—and the consumer is free to pick whichever she chooses.
- Sellers accept all potential purchasers.
- The consumer has adequate knowledge of the product by which to compare the quality of what is offered by each supplier.
- There is a fair degree of predictability of cost to the consumer, making accurate budgeting for expenditures possible.
- The consumer is directly responsible for payment.

Now let's see how the sale and purchase of health care services depart from this model:

What the consumer purchases is often decided by the supplier (i.e., the physician or other health professional). It is estimated that as much as 70 percent of medical service choices are made by the physician rather than the patient, so consumer autonomy is sharply limited. The more serious and complex one's condition, the less the patient is qualified to make purchase decisions on her own.

The product is generally not interchangeable, with such minor exceptions as different generic brands of a medication. In a sense, the physician *is* the product one "buys." You want to go to a physician you trust, and you are advised to check out a tentative choice by finding out where she did her training and whether she is board certified in her specialty. The value of the advice is limited: How many of us know which medical schools and residency (specialist training) programs are among the best and which are among the worst?

Nor are treatments any more interchangeable. The way in which a given condition is treated depends in part on the dominant approach accepted by the local physician community—which research has shown may differ substantially from one town to another. With Dr. A, you may get treatment X or medication Y, whereas with Dr. B, you may get treatment Z or medication W.

Furthermore, the ability even to examine competitors' offerings is greatly inhibited by the fact that you would generally have to pay for an initial office visit with each physician you wished to consider just to find out what he would recommend for your condition. In effect we pay the prospective seller to tell us what he thinks we should buy from him. Health care is, I believe, a unique industry in this respect. Implicit in this point is the fact that the consumer lacks the "product" knowledge that would permit an intelligent choice.

Ironically, in some of the most competitive HMO markets (e.g., southern California, Minneapolis-St. Paul), a perceived need for ever larger scale as a condition of viability has produced such major consolidation that the competition may be becoming monopolistic. If three HMOs divide most of the business, price competition may suffer in health care just as it did two generations ago in the automobile industry, in which a price increase by one of the Big Three was matched by the other two. That's upside down competition!

Many health care market choices have consequences for persons other than the buyer and seller, consequences the market price does not take into account. For example, when a healthy young person foregoes health insurance offered by his employer on a shared-premium basis but later shows up, uninsured, in a hospital ER, everyone else pays his bill through higher insurance costs.

Finally, and perhaps the most peculiar fact of the political economy of health care, is that the consumer—the prospective patient—is not in most cases the true purchaser, although classical economics assumes purchaser and user to be the same person. When it comes to health care, the large majority of Americans are users of services paid for (entirely or partially) by someone else. It's a sort of Alice-in-Wonderland world where words mean what we say they mean, for the true consumer-payer is the employer purchasing coverage to offer as an employee benefit. The prospective patients are more accurately described as the recipients of something a third party (an employer or a government program) has purchased for them. (The first and second parties are the patient and the doctor.) 1997 data show that of 189 million people with private coverage, 165 million are in employment-based plans. The rest, self-employed professionals, small business entrepreneurs, and some families buying coverage for their children, are covered by individual policies.[3] One might call most Americans the beneficiaries of employer largesse, except that economists estimate that much of employer-paid health care coverage is in lieu of higher wages employees might have received in the absence of coverage. Also, employees are paying a steadily increasing share of the premium charged to the employer.

For most Americans in their working years, health care coverage is therefore a privilege of employment, not a right of citizenship. As I write, that privilege is fading: Coverage of workers' dependents by employers is decreasing, as it is for under-65 retirees. The ultimate hole in the tapestry of half-facts that Americans call a competitive health care industry is that it can work only for those who already have coverage. Competition among HMOs cannot provide coverage for the uninsured. And product competition among small businesses provides an incentive for Widget Company A to drop the health insurance it has been providing for its employees, if that means its lower costs will enable it to beat out Widget Company B for a contract. Indeed, current trends provide evidence that the more we try to make the provision of health care follow a competitive market model, the less well the system serves the universal need for access to care. For example:

- Between 1987 and 1995, the percentage of children insured through their parents' workplace dropped from 67 to 59.[4]
- In 1994 only 30 percent of early retirees had coverage from a former employer; in 1988, that figure was 44 percent.[5]

What if the hard edge of global competition continues to provide employers with a reason (or an excuse) to reduce health care employee benefits? If employment simply stops being a reliable source of coverage for most Americans, what would their options be then?

Would individual purchase of health insurance be the solution? Not likely. In the brief period 1989 to 1996, family coverage premiums rose 68 percent for conventional insurance and 58 percent for HMO coverage.

How about a public sector universal social insurance program? Could such a large expansion of the governmental role pass Congress when the center of gravity in American politics has been moving toward what can be called market politics—an assumption that the way for politicians to be reelected is to minimize government and maximize the role of the market?

It is a dilemma—a really big one. Will Americans be compelled to face it? Perhaps not right away. But if downsizing of employer-provided coverage and increased cost-sharing imposed on employees should lead to the number of uninsured passing 50 million people, one can hazard a guess that political pressure may compel consideration of hitherto unacceptable alternatives.

Given the crucial role of the market in the distribution of health care services and Americans' dependence on employer "middlemen" as purchasers on their behalf, we need to make a further incursion into economics at this point. In distributing any good or service, a choice is made: to use a buy-and-sell method where money is the determining factor or an extramarket (nonprofit or government) arrangement in which other factors—need, sympathy, societal gains or losses beyond the buyer and seller—override the usual reliance on market sale. The market/nonmarket choice commonly flows easily from the nature of what is to be distributed.

Elementary economics recognizes three kinds of goods and services: private, public, and mixed goods. A private good is one that you and I cannot use simultaneously. If I consume a slice of bread, it is not available to you. If there is one red convertible in the showroom and you offer more for it than I do, it will be yours. In other words, private goods are rivals: Sale to one person precludes sale to another. And they are divisible: Each unit is separable from the others. When I buy one, you can still buy another unit of the same thing. Goods that are divisible and rival can therefore be distributed on a cash transaction basis. Given a willing seller and a willing buyer, ownership changes hands when the two agree upon a price. The default choice for how to allocate a private good or service is the market, which means simply that we expect such services to be bought and sold for money. Smaller businesses tend to have smaller financial cushions than large corporations, so the financial burden of buying employee health insurance falls more heavily on the former, which explains why a large proportion do not buy employee coverage.

Extramarket distribution requires special justification. The reason we sometimes decide as a society that a rival and excludable good should be allocated on a nonmarket basis can be hinted at by reviewing a little more economics terminology. First, market exchange does not occur simply because a quantity of bread or cars exists and some consumers *want* or even *need* some. As a value-neutral system of analysis, economics is not concerned with "needs"; they represent psychological feelings or social judgments but not anything recognized by a market. No matter how much one may desire something, a transaction does not follow until the desire is backed up by cash. An economic want means desire *plus money*. That combination spells "demand" in economics.

Given these qualities of private goods and markets, we can inquire: Is health care a private good? And the answer is yes—and no.

A *public* good is nonrival: Your consumption of it does not prevent me from also using it. National defense is the classic example. Not even Bill Gates can purchase defense privately, and when government provides it, everyone benefits. Mosquito abatement works the same way. Defense and mosquito control share another trait: They are nonexcludable. If you pay your income tax and I do not, we will both be defended. The mosquito does not know who paid a share of abatement taxes and who did not, so the "free rider" escapes its bites just as well as the good citizen taxpayer.

Is health care a public good? No. So what is it?

Health care is a *mixed* good. It has the properties of a private good—rivalry and excludability. But because U.S. society generally thinks no one should go without needed medical care, Americans have a problem with simply selling

health care like other private goods. Remember that in the market if you cannot pay, you do not get the service. So in some circumstances Americans supplement the workings of the market. Housing subsidies have been a substantial
government program for more than half a century. Public libraries are an out-
standing example of a service collectively provided to ensure equal accessibility
at all income levels.

The most widespread and most universally accepted example of a mixed good
is public education from kindergarten through high school. Americans all share
in K–12 costs for two reasons. First, many millions of children would never receive an education if their parents had to pay full cost (about $6,000 a year). Sec-
ondly, all benefit from this public investment: An educated populace is a bedrock
necessity for a vibrant economy—a stronger point than ever in the information
age. Since Jefferson it has been an article of U.S. political faith that rational decision making in a democracy requires an educated citizenry. Americans adopted
universal public education earlier than European countries and continue today
to lead in this one category of social welfare. Ironically, the public school—probably the most widely accepted of all U.S. institutions—is a leading example of
something U.S. political rhetoric totally rejects: socialism. Public schools are government-owned (albeit by local governmental entities, not the national government), and the teachers and staff are government employees.

In health care Americans do not have anything approaching "socialism" in
this sense on a wide scale, but governmental subsidies do supplement the market in meeting some specific needs. Public health clinics, often operated as outreach efforts of county public hospitals, offer medical services directly to some
indigent patients. Childhood immunization against childhood diseases is publicly subsidized. Many millions of Americans are served by two taxpayer-
financed, extramarket or market-supplementing health care programs:
Medicare, which serves 33 million persons age 65 and over and 5 million disabled individuals, and Medicaid, a joint federal-state program that serves millions (though far from all) of low-income parents and children and underwrites nursing home care for elderly patients who have exhausted their own
resources. Such health care is therefore a mixed good: Its sale could be limited
to those who can afford to pay for it privately, but Americans choose not to so
limit the distribution of its benefits. Put another way, the United States practices collective consumption of health care in certain categories, while leaving
the majority of health care services to private-sector sale and purchase.

Apart from some public health measures, medical care has always been
overwhelmingly a private good in the United States. In Europe, governmentally legislated health insurance for broad segments of the population was ini-

tiated as far back as 1883 in Germany and 1906 in England, but the United States had only minor public supplements until Medicare and Medicaid passed Congress in 1965. The idea of health care being mostly a private responsibility is strongly reinforced by today's widespread belief, particularly among financial pundits, that maximizing the role of the market is the key to success in all matters of economic and social development. So why does government play a prominent role today? The answer lies partly in economics, partly in social ethics.

The economics aspect is the easier part. Health care, like education, has positive externalities. Externalities, in the jargon of economics, are benefits or costs that "spill over"—have effects on persons (third parties) who are neither the buyer (first party) nor seller (second party) in a transaction. Air pollution by cars and factories and water pollution by paper mills are standard examples of negative externalities. The seller and buyer of paper do not willingly include the cost of polluted streams in their transaction. The rest of us feel the harm, and its alleviation is partly paid for by regulating how the producer operates and partly by public expenditures. Similarly, the price of gasoline does not include the cost of air pollution. Our lungs pay part of the price, in a sense, and our taxes pay another part, for regulatory programs to diminish pollution.

Positive externalities turn some private goods and services into quasi-public goods, which means that we—the body politic, the citizenry—see values to protect by ensuring universal distribution of the service in question. I cited the positive externalities of public education earlier, and health presents a similar case. Your good health contributes to my good health, medically and financially. If you stay well, you are unlikely to pass on a transferable medical problem to me and the less we all will have to spend on emergency treatments at public facilities. Better health care reduces the need for other safety net programs: unemployment compensation, sick-day substitutions, and so on. A healthier workforce performs better and loses fewer work days, strengthening the economy for all.

The inability of private transactions to take into account broader consequences affecting third parties produces what economists call market failures. Whether these justify governmental action, either to abate a problem or to enhance the value of a desirable good or service, is not a matter to be determined scientifically. The answer depends on the social value one attaches to the matter at hand, although the writings of many economists imply that a difficult burden of proof faces any claim that government should intervene in a market.

(Here is an interesting question for political science students: Do political scientists, because they have been attracted to the study of government as a career choice, tend easily to accept government interventions into markets? Do they simply trust governments, just as economists tend to trust markets, which are the institutions they have chosen to spend a lifetime studying? These questions are intriguing in light of the importance of politico-economic factors in the analysis of almost all public policy problems.)

Is There an Ethical "Right" to Health Care?

From quite another position, the argument for supplementing the market mode of supplying care rests upon extra-economic rationales. These rationales range from ethical and philosophical propositions debated among academics, particularly philosophers and medical ethicists, to man-in-the-street reactions. These arguments lie in a different realm from that of economics, one alien to enshrining a process—the market mechanism—as equal in importance to the societal goal of universal health care access.

Americans are fond of proclaiming rights. After all, the Bill of Rights stands with the Declaration of Independence and the Constitution as one of the nation's sacred documents. Americans have also unfortunately developed the custom of loosely using the phrase, ". . . a right to. . . ." They elevate to the status of moral rights those that are merely legal: They exist only because a legislative body has created a program with benefits to which one has a "right" (i.e., a legal entitlement) if one meets specified criteria. Medicare, Supplementary Security Income, and Medicaid are standard examples. Even strongly held expectations that may not have legislative backing—such as being able to appeal to an independent arbiter a managed care's decision not to pay for a certain expensive procedure—are thought of (by the patient) as rights.

If such usage does not totally debase the meaning of a hallowed term in this nation's constitutional pantheon, it does at least confuse public discussion of who is to pay the bills. For example, a 1988 Harris poll found 91 percent approval for the statement that "everybody should have the right to the best possible healthcare—as good as a millionaire gets." Easy to say, but what does it mean?

- That doctors and hospitals should ignore the existence or extent of a patient's insurance coverage or the content of his wallet?
- That government should underwrite universal health care coverage—say by universalizing Medicare, which now ensures acute care for the over-65 population?

- That my insurance plan or HMO must allow me to pick the most notable specialist at an academic medical center when I need some complicated procedure, no matter whether that physician is on the plan's list or not?
- That Congress or state legislatures should fashion a legally binding "Patients' Bill of Rights?" So far, Congress has created only one universal legal right: A 1986 law requires that hospitals treat persons whose life depends on immediate attention, at least until their condition has been stabilized. A 1997 presidential commission charged with drafting a patients' bill of rights could come to no unanimous agreement, and although President Clinton issued an executive order to extend the panel's recommendations to Medicare beneficiaries, those recommendations included no suggestions for enforcement.

Is your reaction the complex one of initial agreement with the claim of a right to the highest quality care that money can buy, followed by a "Well, I don't mean quite that" when confronted by the situations hypothesized?

From whatever motivation and rationale, the United States does have a variety of medical entitlements, related to age, income, disease, and other factors. Yet these instances of treating health care as a public good or engaging in collective consumption offer far less than a complete set of legal rights. The specific categories are beneficiaries for whom there is the greatest political sympathy (children covered under Medicaid beyond their parents' eligibility), or who have the greatest political clout (the over-65 age group, which combines a high voter turnout rate with political sympathy), or who have just been politically clever and lucky: those with end stage renal disease and needing kidney dialysis. End stage renal disease is the only specific disease for which Medicare eligibility has been created for persons under age 65. How did it come about? Wheeling kidney patients into a congressional hearing room did the trick, not an objective analysis of medical priorities.

Turning from the concrete realm of legislated entitlements (legal rights), let's now sample some contemporary intellectual scaffolding for an abstract right to health care. Because economics as a discipline explicitly—even proudly, some might say—avoids discussing values, public debates in the United States about health care reform often fail to deal with issues of justice and fairness. For those, we have to shift to the academic discipline of philosophy. Norman Daniels grapples directly with the value issues embedded in the health care system. He asserts a moral right to health care as a requirement of justice. The starting point for his argument is to embrace what is perhaps the most basic of American public values: equality of opportunity. To do more than make rhetorical obeisance to this most widely shared attribute, we must be functioning normally in terms of health, among other things. We may have unequal talents, but it is only our talents, not extraneous conditions stemming from race, gender, lack of education *or poor health status*, that may justly differentiate our rewards.

On this basis, Daniels (with two colleagues) published *Benchmarks of Fairness for Health Care Reform* to be used in making comparative assessment of the existing system and various alternatives.[6] These spell out some specific assertions for what a right to health care should mean today:

- Universal access: Everyone is covered; when one moves or changes jobs, portability and continuity of coverage are guaranteed; maldistributions of personnel and facilities are minimized, as are barriers of language, culture, and social class.
- Comprehensive and uniform benefits: All medically necessary, effective services are covered.
- Equitable financing: Community-rated premiums are used (i.e., insurance premiums are set by average needs of the population in a given area, rather than better rates for the healthiest and higher rates for those whose health is most at risk); payment is made according to ability to pay, either through public financing from progressive taxes or subsidized premiums.
- Value for money: Clinical efficacy is created through an emphasis on primary care and prevention; under- and overutilization is minimized.
- Value for money: Financial efficiency is created by minimizing administrative costs.

An effective right to health care would exist if a system got high marks on all of these criteria. How, then, do present trends in what is called the health care delivery system stack up? Daniels' and his colleagues' assessment is not an optimistic one. They found that 2 million people lost health insurance between 1994 and the printing of their 1996 book. In terms of a right to health care, how many people have insurance coverage is obviously the most important single marker. They found that maldistribution had gotten worse, in terms of closed rural hospitals and a lack of facilities in poorer urban areas; however, they found an improvement in that Medicaid patients were being mainstreamed into HMOs, in which they got the same care as non-Medicaid enrollees. Equity in financing had worsened in an ever stronger movement away from community rating, and there had been no movement at all toward financing coverage based on ability to pay. Value for money had improved, they asserted, through a greater emphasis on primary care (versus using specialists). They also saw a favorable trend in reduced overutilization of medical care, through managed care's reductions in hospitalizations and research efforts to study outcomes as a way of developing physician guidelines that may reduce both over- and underutilization. Finally, they found no improvement in the proportion of health care expenditures going into administrative costs rather than medical care, although they did see a plus in the hard bargaining of employer and HMO purchasers of care to reduce payments to the hospitals and physicians providing services. (Some commentators fear a minus if provider incomes drop to a point at which hospitals discontinue services that may be needed in the community but do not pay their way, especially as community nonprofit hospitals are bought out by for-profit chains.)

Such assessments cannot really be measured quantitatively, in my view, but are worth doing to sketch point-in-time profiles of various aspects of the health care system. At the least, this study makes it clear that the United States has some distance to go before a medical and financial right to health care will have been secured for all Americans.

The approach just summarized justifies a government mandate for health coverage as a necessary means to make equal opportunity a practical reality. And equal opportunity is the American way of combining individualism and egalitarianism. So, paradoxically, collective action underwrites strengthening individual self-reliance.

An approach based on a somewhat different set of considerations is taken by another academic philosopher, Larry R. Churchill. The crux of his argument is that we are all in this together:

> All share a common human vulnerability to disease, disability, and death. All of us face the future without knowing when or how urgently we will need health services. We all support through tax dollars the creation and maintenance of the various institutions of health care. . . . All have a stake in a healthy populace above and beyond the stake each has in his or her personal health.[7]

He develops this social solidarity theme by pointing out that no one can predict what health services he may need, or when, or what they will cost. Americans all know that being insured by one's employer is a precarious privilege today and that unexpected gaps in coverage can occur in the best of health plans. One of two primary goals Churchill sets for the health care system, therefore, is *security*, freedom from fear that one's health needs may go unad-

dressed or cause one to go bankrupt. As a second primary objective he pro-
poses the principle of *solidarity,* "the sense of community that emerges from
acknowledgment of shared benefits and burdens. . . . Security is not attainable
without solidarity, and solidarity is meaningless unless it ensures the security
of each individual."[8]

The solidarity argument is also used by ethicist Daniel Callahan to describe
the European health care model, in contrast to the rights model developed in
the United States.[9] In his view, the rights approach opens the way to unlimited
claims and excessive demands. The solidarity model, he argues, is accepted in
the United States in the areas of public education, fire and police protection,
and national defense, but Americans have not applied this thinking to health
care, with Medicare as a major exception. In Europe it is the social solidarity
principle—we're all in this together—that underlies the universal health insurance systems developed in the past century. Combined with centralized national budgeting, this system also allows a limit to be set on the extent of coverage provided, which a rights orientation finds harder to do. Callahan suggests
that "a combined rights and solidarity approach would work best."[10]

So now we have two philosophic arguments whose realization would necessitate legislative enactments and a strong governmental presence. Does this
mean that one must have either a market system for health care or a public sector system? Not necessarily. Most nations have mixtures, in varying degrees, of
private market and public, governmental elements. All except the United States
and South Africa, however, have used government to ensure universal coverage.

One thing is clear: The existing pattern in the United States, in which one-
seventh of the population has access to care only on an emergency or charitable basis, is far from fulfilling what Americans overwhelmingly tell pollsters
they believe should be available for those needing health care. In the next
chapter, I'll ask, "How did Americans get themselves in such a pickle—a loose,
unplanned system of health care services that generally uses a wallet biopsy as
a test of eligibility for treatment, despite nearly unanimous protestations that
they want everyone to have access to the best health care? And, what are the
defining characteristics of the received system—a system undergoing very
rapid change?"

2

The Accidental System

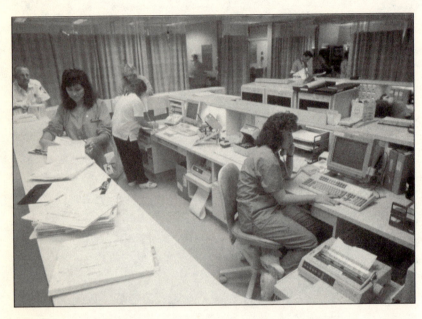

Emergency department nurses' station. Photo courtesy of Stock Boston, © 1994 by
Charles Gupton, reprinted with permission.

Netscape Navigator is a system. Municipal water purification is a system. Criminal justice is a system. Each comprises a set of planned parts and their interrelationships, which is how we generally think of a system. In most industrial countries, health care delivery ("delivery" is the health world's jargon for how professional services reach the patient) is also in substantial measure a system in that sense. European nations passed laws during the first part of this century to organize their health care institutions and financing, whether through public institutions or by mandating policies to be followed in the private sector.

In the United States, however, health care is an accidental system, especially in its financial relationships. It has not been purposefully created but inadvertently developed. It results from Americans' ideological preference for decentralization and for avoiding the use of government—and is a byproduct of an economic management decision made during World War II (1939–1945) with absolutely no thought that it would shape the entire health care delivery pattern for decades to come.

The Early Years

To profile the system, I have to start early in this century with the surprising fact—if you, as I, tend to assume that the institutional patterns we grew up with have always been there—that until about 1900, hospitals were mostly for the poor. They were essentially almshouse infirmaries, and their patients were less likely to be cured than to die there. Pre-1900 hospitals were beds, bedpans, and sinks—a far cry from the high-tech, *Chicago Hope* or *ER* picture of electronic testing devices and teams of doctors and nurses performing surgical miracles.

Germ theory gained acceptance in the 1880s, as did Joseph Lister's concepts of antiseptic procedures. With development of x-rays in 1895, doctors began to do many more operations, with much greater safety than before. These innovations and more treatments of clear benefit encouraged private patients of middle class or better means to use hospitals, which had become safer than one's home. A better-than-even chance of benefiting from care, thanks to technological and biomedical approaches to disease treatment, meant two things by the 1920s. First, receiving health care was becoming a common expectation. Second, costs of care rose, partly through more frequent use and partly through the proliferation of new equipment and new kinds of medicines.

Effective care meant more expensive care. How were we to respond to that mix? In 1883, Germany's Chancellor Bismarck instituted a system of government-sponsored though privately operated health care as a way (ironically) of deflecting socialist political pressures. In 1906, Great Britain incorporated private "sickness societies" into a limited early form of national health insurance for low income workers. Other nations acted in similar manner, but the United States, in keeping with its private, individual-oriented approach to social needs, began to develop prepaid hospital insurance only in the 1920s. A squeeze was catching the middle class, whose incomes were too high for charity care in public wards yet too low to afford the large, unpredictable expenditures that medical care could now entail.

In 1929, on the eve of the Great Depression, Dr. Justin Ford Kimball, administrator of the Baylor University Hospital in Dallas, Texas, started a plan under which one could prepay up to 21 days of hospitalization per year through an insurance premium of 50 cents a month. From this seed has grown the mighty acorn of private health insurance coverage. Stimulated by the increasing numbers who could not pay their hospital bills as the economic decline worsened, the American Hospital Association (AHA) created the Blue Cross system of nonprofit, but private, coverage plans, and by 1940 over 4 million people were enrolled. Blue Shield, covering physician payments, came later. AHA sponsorship gave health insurance a pro-hospital bias from the beginning. This bias led to such unanticipated and costly consequences as the practice of physicians putting their patients into a hospital to establish eligibility for insurance payment of tests and x-rays that could have been done as well on an outpatient basis.

Probably the single most significant event in shaping the U.S. system came in 1943, one that would leave a substantial segment of the population without health care coverage right up to the present day. In World War II, booming industrial production was causing incomes to rise. Wage and price controls were put in effect to prevent runaway inflation, but war production needs had nearly eliminated many civilian goods from the shelves. Unable to bargain for wage increases, unions pushed for fringe benefits—and corporations making high profits and fearing any disruption acceded to the demands. When these benefits were ruled to be permissible under the wage controls, they took off, and health care coverage was an immediate beneficiary, along with pensions. Because these benefits were tax free, their popularity increased with workers.

By the end of the war, Blue Cross had 19 million hospitalization subscribers, a number that quadrupled by 1950. Fifty-four million workers also had surgery coverage by then. Of course these figures included a wide variation in plans, some with excellent, some with meager coverage. With widespread hospital coverage for workers, dramatic changes in medical practices took place: Birthing moved from the home (50 percent in 1935) to the hospital (96 percent 20 years later). That change exemplifies an important but insufficiently realized causal influence of financing patterns upon actual delivery of medical care. As we shall see, that influence continues to be a decisive factor, one causing much turbulence among medical professionals, patients, and politicians as I write.

Such is the pace of change in health care that hardly had the hospitals achieved a pinnacle of success when the movement toward outpatient treatment began. From the 1950s onward, there has been a shift—gradual at first, then picking up the pace in the 1990s—toward outpatient settings, with freestanding (i.e., neither physically nor organizationally part of a hospital) surgicenters and urgent care clinics bursting into public and media consciousness by the early 1990s. For example, between 1980 and 1993, the rate of inguinal hernia repairs done on a hospital inpatient basis dropped from 483,000 to 96,000.[1]

HMOs and Prospective Payment

The most significant organizational development of the last quarter century is the rise since the early 1970s of what are now called managed care entities— HMOs (health maintenance organizations), PPOs (preferred provider organizations), POSs (point of service organizations), and yet other acronymous inventions. The defining characteristic of an HMO has been to combine the insurance and service-providing functions into a single organization, with subscribers paying a fixed sum per person (hence called a capitation fee). In exchange, the HMO promises to provide any needed type and amount of service, within a contractually defined scope of benefits.

The revolution in health care did not originate, nor does it receive its primary continuing impetus, as a spontaneous business strategy. Spiraling health care expenditures by private employers and governments, federal and state, did the job. Between 1970 and 1980, employer expenditures for employee benefits

(85 percent of which was for health insurance) went up 352 percent; in the mid-1980s, premiums rose 6–8 percent annually; then into double digits in the early 1990s.² Medicare and Medicaid expenditures followed a similar trajectory. In addition, these growing costs began just as the postwar economy started to slow down. In consequence, the overall thrust of effective national concern began to switch from, How can we ensure coverage for all Americans? to, How can we control these ballooning costs?

In 1973, President Richard M. Nixon helped provide one answer when he pushed through legislation to encourage the formation of HMOs, even putting up federal funds to help new ones get started and requiring employers to include an HMO in offerings to employees if one was operating in the firm's area. His health advisers were persuaded that moving medical care from the cottage industry stage of individual practitioners to that of large-scale enterprises organized on business competition principles would reign in costs. As so often happens with major policy initiatives, the unanticipated consequences turned out to be more significant than the intended ones. Nixon's encouragement did not produce an immediate groundswell of HMO growth; however, capitation, the new way of paying for health care, became the unofficial doctrine of cost containment efforts, ready to seize the dominant position when the opportunity presented. That came in the 1980s.

Capitation has more recently been extended in the private sector from the subscribers to the professionals who provide the actual services (therefore called "providers," for convenience when lumping together physicians, nurses, other allied health professionals, and even hospitals). The HMO thus passes on its risks to those it contracts with to do the treatments. The hospital or the physician now often receives a fixed sum per patient, sometimes with supplementary arrangements that increase compensation if actual costs for the patients of a group of physicians are lower than the budgeted expectation.

A payment fixed in advance for a specific treatment or a per diem hospital stay is called a prospective payment, and the main push for this came from the public sector in the Reagan administration. Learning from a system initiated in New Jersey, Congress in 1983 instructed the Health Care Financing Administration (HCFA—pronounced "hickfa" by those who have to deal with it all the time) to use a system of Diagnostic Related Groups (DRGs) for hospital payments covering nearly 500 conditions. For instance, DRG 79 was for respiratory infections, 103 for a heart transplant, and 410 for chemotherapy. On the basis of an economic analysis of the cost and length of stay typical for each DRG, a payment fee was assigned, as opposed to the older system of adding up charges for every discrete element of the services and materials provided by the hospital.

DRG payments are for the hospital only; physician payments for services in the hospital are separate. To control burgeoning physician charges for Medicare patients, another prospective payment system (PPS) to cover physician fees was introduced beginning in 1992. Called RBRVS (little can be done in government without an acronym), which means Resource Based Relative Value System, it assigns a numerical value (translated into dollars and cents at an annually determined rate) to each of several thousand services performed by physicians. For example, a comprehensive initial visit with an internist has one value, a brief continuing visit another, and every procedure, whether surgical or testing for a suspected condition, has its own value. Interestingly, although there are about 7,000 categories of physician services, the top twenty medical services accounted for 35 percent of all spending for physician services in 1990. Anticipating that doctors might "game the system" by increasing the number of services they performed, HCFA developed another policy response: a soft limit (Volume Performance Standard, or VPS) on the annual total dollar volume of Medicare payments to physicians. Nowhere is the truism that every solution carries within it the seeds of a new problem more valid than in health care!

DRGs, the physician fee schedule, and HMO capitation are all forms of prospective payment, and all of them are ways for a health care organization, whether business or government program, to gain greater predictability in its efforts to balance income and expenditures. Prospective payment is more fundamental than it may seem on first acquaintance, because all forms of prospective payment reverse physician and hospital incentives. In the traditional medical world of fee-for-service (FFS) medicine, the more my doctor does for me, the more he may charge; the longer I stay in the hospital and the more pieces of equipment and expendable supplies I use, the more the hospital charges me. Reversing the incentives means that in the managed care world the *less* that is done, the more net income the organization retains. For example, if the average hospital stay for my condition is six days and a DRG rate is set on that basis, but I am fit enough to be sent home in three, the hospital will make money. If I have to stay ten days, it will lose. The HMO receives a fixed sum per subscriber (that's what capitation means), but its own costs vary. The lower its costs, the more of its gross income it retains. For a nonprofit entity, that surplus can be used to upgrade equipment and improve services; for a profit-seeking, publicly held corporation, it also means being able to pay dividends to shareholders.

Are the new ways harmful to patients? Not necessarily: *Over*treatment has been a problem in the fee-for-service sector. Are the new ways then helpful?

Not necessarily: They may swing from overuse to underuse of medical resources. It is a medico-economic dilemma, it seems, and certainly a politico-economic problem as demands are made to protect consumer-patients from being caught on either horn of the dilemma. (See Chapter 7.)

The Public Sector: Niche Health Care

Medicare, Medicaid, the Indian Health Service, veterans hospitals, and health services in the active military are all areas of financing or direct provision of medical services by government. Each program has been created by legislators to take care of some segment of the population lacking market access (in plain English, not having enough money). It is public policy by incremental niche. Each program has been created at a different time, in a specific political context, to respond to a particular need. The system did not emerge from one big public or congressional debate; it is the result of an accretion of bits and pieces.

The Social Security legislation of 1935—in the heart of the Great Depression—included grants to the states for maternal and child health. A broader effort was urged by some, but President Franklin D. Roosevelt feared that old age insurance, the primary goal, would be lost if the same bill tried to include health insurance. At that time, California and New York had their own medical programs for the very poor, with public hospitals and clinics. In 1950, amendments to the Social Security Act began to provide public assistance payments to health providers as part of welfare. In 1960, the Kerr-Mills Act responded to apparently increasing public sentiment favoring government action to help seniors meet the cost of health care needs. It created open-ended federal cost sharing for state programs, but the states were not required to have a program. A state deciding to participate did not have to meet any minimum benefit provisions, except that its program had to extend throughout the state (so that southern states could not exclude predominantly black counties) and there were to be no enrollment fees. The state response was slow, and as 1964 began only 29 states had Kerr-Mills programs, most of minimal scope.

The states doing the most on their own got the bulk of the funding. In 1963, 65 percent of the money went to only five states, covering only 32 percent of the over-65 population. The low-income states could not afford to start programs, even with an 80 percent match. As so often is the case in American federalism, the states make fine experimental laboratories, but the national government has to act if the successful experiments are to become uniformly available across the nation.

As the inadequacy of the Kerr-Mills approach became clear, the social insurance concept embedded in Social Security pensions received increasing attention as a model for health care. President John F. Kennedy had endorsed the Medicare concept in 1961 in a health message to Congress, and after a Democratic landslide in the 1964 elections, President Lyndon B. Johnson achieved success and signed Medicare and Medicaid into law on July 30, 1965.

The broad scope of this legislation was itself an accidental by-product of last-minute political horse trading, not the culmination of a carefully worked out legislative agenda. As the 1965 congressional session began, the Johnson administration was pushing a hospital care bill that would not cover physicians' services at all, fearing that AMA opposition to that part would kill everything. A Republican alternative provided hospital and physician benefits as an expansion of the Kerr-Mills approach, to cover only very low income seniors. A bitter battle was anticipated.

What actually happened surprised everyone. Representative Wilbur Mills, chair of the House Ways and Means Committee and therefore a crucial player, treated the competing proposals not as either-or, but as complementary. After some complicated maneuvering, the two elements were joined as Part A (hospitals) and Part B (physicians), both applying to all seniors as a social insurance rather than a welfare measure. In his case study, *The Politics of Medicare,* Theodore R. Marmor termed this result "a model of unintended consequences."[3]

To cover all of the aged, without a means test, was a bold stroke by the standards of American political expectations for government programs. To a European, it must have seemed minimal, for continental nations had long covered their entire populations, not just their elderly. Even in the United States, proposals for universal health insurance (UHI) had surfaced strongly, though briefly, before World War I, and President Harry S. Truman sent to Congress the first presidential message ever on health care in November 1945. He made it a major 1948 political goal to "remove the money barrier between illness and therapy, . . . [and thus] protect all our people equally . . . against ill health." By the end of 1949, however, UHI was politically dead for that time, killed by a campaign against "socialized medicine." The campaign was developed by a California public relations firm, Whitaker and Baxter, and included many cutting-edge techniques for grassroots lobbying. For example, they suggested that county medical societies contact the personal physician of every congressman and senator in their state and ask them to send a personal letter to the legislator urging defeat of "compulsory health insurance legislation." Whitaker and Baxter provided form letters but suggested that the medical society secretary rewrite and personalize each letter. The proponents, with expenditures of $38,000, could not prevail against the opponents' lobbying fund of $2.25 million, no matter how often it was explained that government payment to a private doctor of his "usual and customary" fee hardly constituted socialism.

When Truman's proposals were killed, proponents of UHI regrouped around the elderly, a high proportion of whom were clearly of low income. Social Security pensions were still small and in the 1950s had not been extended to all categories of workers. The over-65 population had no employer coverage, and they could not be told to go out and earn the money with which to buy private insurance.

So Medicare came into being to cover the elderly with a dignified social insurance program unrelated to income. In a companion bill passed at the same time, some of the under-65 poor (not all, by any means) were given Medicaid—a less-dignified, means-tested program. The poor and the elderly are thus the major niches in civilian, government health programs. Niche development continues to dominate the U.S. approach to health care problems; they are solved seriatim as they reach the media and political surface and demand attention by elected officials. Since 1973, Medicare has also covered persons permanently and totally disabled and end stage renal disease patients.

Medicaid is a patchwork of provisions passed over the years, some restricting and some expanding eligibility. Mothers and children on welfare and very elderly poor people requiring nursing home care have been the two largest categories of eligibility. (For a more detailed program description, see Chapter 5.)

Because Medicare and Medicaid are tax-financed programs, their costs are far more concentrated on one federal and fifty state governments and therefore more visible than the larger private sector costs spread across thousands of payers. For that reason, the entitlements battle will be high on the political agenda over the next few years as the baby boomers reach Medicare age. (An entitlement means simply that some level of government has obligated itself to pay for certain services if you have met statutory eligibility criteria; e.g., have reached age 65 for Medicare entitlement.)

In an interesting deviation from the usual hand-wringing over entitlement costs, health economist Uwe Reinhardt has argued that Americans should not worry so much about aggregate health care costs increasing, even rapidly. He points out that Americans would celebrate the economic growth if auto sales rose at a double digit rate, so why not do so when health care costs have a robust growth? After all, more jobs are created and more incomes are earned in health care as expenditures rise. The political difference is simply, but crucially, that Americans accept all sorts of private price increases with only a momentary grumble but greet an increase in taxes with a vehement "No! No! No!" That's the way U.S. market ideology works. In addition, other economists point out that because health care is largely paid for by third parties, it does not meet a market test of competitive value to individual consumers. That is, its opportunity cost is not measured: Individual consumers do not compare the health care they receive against the other goods and services, private or public, that could have been purchased with the same funds.

Niche-ism, if we may call it that, fits the American political predilection for piecemeal policy making, and it has unquestionably expanded health care for some citizens and for some health problems: dialysis for renal failure patients and rapid increases for research budgets aimed at a disease in the news, be it AIDS, or breast cancer, or prostate cancer. A more basic decision that health care should be divorced from income is, however, the only way the largest empty niche of all—the 43.4 million Americans totally lacking health insurance[4]—can be filled.

Partial, self-interested planning also characterizes the accidental system. Each segment plans for itself in the competition for the dollar, and much of the effort in recent years has been designed to shift costs to the other guy. In fact, "cost shifting" came to be part of the basic lingo of the field in the 1980s, and a rather clear cycle developed.

The employer suddenly awakened to rapidly increasing employee benefit costs as its health insurance contractor increased rates annually to pay for the medical inflation it was feeling itself. The employer demanded a slowing of the rate of increase. To accomplish that without reducing its own income, the health insurer demanded discounts from the hospitals and physicians this employer's plan used. The providers then tried—successfully for some time—to shift the costs not so fully met from that plan's reimbursements onto other payers whose insurers were not yet pressing as hard. In the early part of the 1980s, the federal government was the "shiftee," one might say. Medicare had not learned to play the new game and was still paying "usual and customary" charges, roughly defined in practice as whatever rates a provider had been able to charge in its locality. DRGs and fee controls after 1986 made it harder to shift costs onto Uncle Sam, and Medicare's rate of expenditure increase began to fall. As HMOs came to dominate the scene, the pressure for discounts in the private sector intensified, and in the mid-1990s the rate of increase in private health spending fell to single-digit levels. By 1998, however, the trajectory was again turning upward. As I write, the question is whether there is much more cost saving to be made by squeezing providers, without endangering quality, or whether some new and different approach to cost control will have to be taken.

The federal government also concentrates on saving itself money; for example, Clinton's 1997 Medicare and Medicaid changes will cost states and the elderly more money. No one is planning, *or can plan,* for the system as a whole, because it is in fact a multiplicity of partial systems with no overall structure and no way to set an overall budget. Such structure and budget are what other nations do have, and two of the major reasons they control costs better.

A $14 billion National Institutes of Health budget is an important though not highly visible part of the system. It probably deserves more attention, because it may be a wild card. Some health care cost analyses have identified technological change as the largest single factor making it difficult to restrain a long-term cost increase trend. To the extent that federally sponsored research produces new drugs, procedures, or equipment—or that NIH basic research gives private firms a basis for product development—the United States is sometimes achieving new benefits that simultaneously add new costs to the system. Should the national government slow its rapidly increasing health care research budget (knowing that the private sector will not pick up the slack, because basic research cannot be made proprietary)? Such a move would reduce the rate of health expenditure increase, although it would also likely slow down achievement of some medically beneficial treatments. That's another dilemma to think about.

Where Are Current Trends Leading?

In 1994, UHI was briefly resuscitated with much fanfare in President Clinton's ill-fated Health Security Plan. When it was shot down in Congress (see Chapter 3), the political health game changed back to incrementalism. Although not immediately recognized in the aftermath of defeat, that plan did put some health care delivery system problems on the active agenda, for even strong opponents of the administration's proposal conceded that some reforms were needed. Portability (being assured of continued coverage when one changed jobs) was a major one. Being eligible for coverage despite having a preexisting condition (a medical problem one has before becoming insured that may well require treatment after enrollment) was another. These issues were addressed in a 1997 Democratic liberal–Republican moderate partnership, the Kassebaum–Kennedy bill. Other 1996 legislation gave mental health services parity with the rest of acute care coverage and created a trial run of medical savings accounts (MSAs), into which one makes tax-free contributions that can be taken out for ordinary medical expenses, while buying an insurance policy to cover catastrophic (i.e., very costly) incidents.

Piecemeal changes did not stop then. The 1997 Balanced Budget Act (BBA) saved money for the baby boomer–threatened Medicare hospital fund (Part A) by switching most home health expenses to Part B (thus gradually shifting more of the costs onto the beneficiaries in the form of higher Part B premiums), and it encouraged rural HMOs by allowing higher capitation rates and by reducing the rate of increase in funding for more urban HMOs.

An enlarged cafeteria of nontraditional programs, given the sexy title of Medicare + Choice, was also incorporated in the BBA. As Part C of Medicare, it includes PPOs; point of service (POS) plans; provider service organizations (PSOs), health delivery organizations put together directly by physicians and hospitals to avoid the middleman of HMOs; and three conceptually far-reaching new programs. (See Chapter 5, "How Many Kinds of Medicare?")

Health care reform proposals and discussions continue to appear with regularity, with two very divergent meanings. To many health policy wonks and liberal observers, reform means moving toward universal coverage. To employers, managed care firms, state governors, and Medicare planners, reform means tightening cost controls to the point at which the rate of health care cost increase is no higher than the overall rate of inflation. Many—presumably all—would hope for both, and a 1988 proposal by President Clinton to allow the near-elderly (ages 55–64) to "buy in" to Medicare shows that the cost-containment imperative does not totally foreclose initiatives to expand coverage.

Since the late 1970s, several hundred community hospitals have disappeared and some 800 public and nonprofit hospitals have converted to for-profit status. Giant for-profit hospital chains have arisen, the largest having 350 hospitals. Along with consolidation has gone integration: cooperative arrangements of more or less formality linking hospitals, subacute facilities (nursing homes, rehabilitation units, etc.), and physician groups.

More startling than hospital oligopolization has been the rapid consolidation of physicians' practices into large groups. Hanging out one's shingle as a solo practitioner has been a declining scenario for decades, but the shift toward group practices has accelerated. Here, too, the market mode is rapidly changing the basic context of medical practice. Physician groups that had been local partnerships are now being bought by national physician management companies, with the doctors sometimes becoming shareholder employees of for-profit entities. As physician groups and physician-hospital alliances begin attempting to compete with HMOs, they of course need business management expertise that is not taught in medical schools. So management service organizations (MSOs) develop to handle the contracts that are now the lifeline of physician groups, thus putting M.B.A.s into leadership positions in M.D. organizations.

The public at large may not be fully aware of these industrializing trends, but many people are acutely aware of the alleged consequences that they read in the paper or learn of through television: having difficulty getting an appointment, discovering that your primary care physician of last month is no longer part of the "team," learning that your physician cannot authorize the tests she told you yesterday she thought you needed, or being sent home from the hospital before you feel ready.

Ours is truly a mixed economy, and health care is a very central part of the mix. Taken together, the developments covered in this chapter demonstrate that public policy and private markets intersect continuously as both sectors face problems for which customers or constituents demand solutions. Both their successes and the unanticipated consequences lead to new problems, and another round begins. This situation is true in all health care (and other large) systems, but perhaps more so in the United States because it lacks even some basic, agreed-upon parameters governing access to health services. The U.S. system is a jury-rigged, private-public, market-extra market multiplicity of partial subsystems.

As prospective patients, all U.S. citizens have a personal stake in the developing pattern, but the language of the nation's interest group-oriented political system largely reserves the term "stakeholders" for those with an organized financial or professional interest in what happens. At a 1997 conference about the impact of recent changes in health care delivery, I heard assessments of what was happening to every such interest—but very little about the net impact of all the changes on the ultimate stakeholders, the patients. Consolidation of providers, an aging and ever larger population, and an accidental system that in 1996 spent $3,898 per person on health care all combine to make health care more and more a battle of behemoths. So it is time now to ask: Who are the actors in this drama? What institutions wield power and influence? What are the rules of engagement in this continuing politico-economic battle? Are American political practices and governmental institutions up to the task of setting guidelines for a trillion-dollar industry that literally revolves around life and death issues?

3

The Stakeholders and the Policy Process

President Bill Clinton holds up a proposed health security identification card while outlining his plan for health care reform to a joint session of Congress, September 22, 1993, on Capitol Hill. Photo courtesy of AP Photo/Ron Edmonds, reprinted with permission.

The Clinton Health Plan Debacle and Its Aftermath

On September 22, 1993, President Clinton, addressing a joint session of Congress, waved a mock-up Health Security card in front of a national television audience and made an extremely well received appeal for universal health coverage. On September 26, 1994, Senate Majority Leader George Mitchell officially declared the president's plan legislatively dead.

What happened in between? Political postmortems inherently lack scientific precision, but this debacle has more than its share of diverse, even contradictory, explanations. A quick review of them perhaps illustrates the mixed state of political science analysis as much as it does Clinton's problems of political strategy.

Some problems seem clear in almost all commentaries:

- A 500-person White House planning group was too large and was headed by a management expert lacking political savvy and operating without seeking input from politically experienced staff or congressional insiders.
- Congressional leadership sent the Clinton plan to five standing committees instead of putting together a special committee structure.
- Since the Watergate era, the structure of Congress had been "atomized" and leadership made more difficult. Opponents of reform were well financed and well organized, whereas supporters were fragmented into blocs advocating specific approaches different from Clinton's.
- The Clinton plan, which in one version ran to 1,342 pages, was too complex to be understood (or at least was not explained well enough and often enough while under attack).

Note that those explanations of failure are matters of internal structure and conventional interest group theory. Political science has for half a century had two dicta that apply here. First, it is far easier to defend than to change the status quo. Second, interest groups often have a "veto" over changes they disfavor.

Some commentators, however, see the fatal factor as located in the larger political environment:

- Clinton was only a 43 percent presidential victor in 1992.
- There was no ardently pro-reform, politically potent group constituency.
- There had not been a lengthy legislative gestation period of bills worked on over a number of years (as there had been for Medicare in 1965).
- The need was not obvious to enough of the middle class voters who enjoyed employee benefit coverage.
- The opposition had a simple, single objective—to stop change— whereas the pro-reform groups were splintered into support of several quite different approaches to universal coverage.
- Finally, the opposition spent more on manipulating public opinion and was more sophisticated in what it did than the Clinton administration and its supporting groups.

Overall, explanations for the steep rise and fall of the universal coverage initiative fall into two categories. One is the traditional nuts-and-bolts political science lens of interest groups and congressional committees and their procedures—the internal view. The other emphasizes what we may call the macroenvironment of public opinion polling, television commercials, and the mass media's political coverage. That coverage largely ignores explaining the substance of policy disputes but instead focuses hard on the horse race dimension: Who won a point today; who lost a point today.

In an incisive postmortem of the Clinton plan, Jacob S. Hacker develops an argument that cuts across both of these dimensions. He focuses on the agenda-setting stage of policy making and how its shaping can affect legislative consideration and public opinion reaction to a major bill. He emphasizes that although traditional interest group power was very much on the minds of the bill's authors and although few presidents (if any) have been as poll conscious as Clinton, the intellectual origins and conceptual design of the Health Security Plan created what proved to be the crucial stumbling blocks.[1]

In the 1950s, political scientists discerned at the heart of much policy making a pattern of "iron triangles": collaborations among an executive branch bureau, a congressional committee or subcommittee, and an organized economic interest group. The voting public was seen as peripheral to much policy making, and most issues did not involve much intellectual innovation, scientific or academic. In 1978, Hugh Heclo coined the term "issue networks" to note a change toward broadened sources of policy ideas. As natural and social science data and concepts revealed (and sometimes created) complexities not previously realized, the groupings that devised policy proposals came to include academics and other professionals in every sphere. The Clinton health plan carried these tendencies an additional step: It was developed largely out of a rather esoteric set of propositions applying neoclassical economics and an ideological gloss favoring competitive markets rather than government as the "of course" way to approach societal problems.

Alain C. Enthoven, a Stanford University business economist, has been a major protagonist for what he (and others, following his lead) call the managed competition approach, with writings over a quarter-century advocating a "Consumer-Choice Health Plan."[2] A 1989 version has been pushed by what became known among health policy wonks as the Jackson Hole group, an influential mix of free-market economists and insurance industry executives whose firms were developing HMO "products."

Proposals published in academic journals by professional economists are not the stuff out of which politically sexy legislative proposals are usually formed. Managed competition gained public leverage, however, when the *New York Times* ran a series of endorsing editorials by an editorial board member, himself an economics Ph.D., Michael Weinstein. In this instance, a major media element could not be accused of just taking note of who was winning and who losing the battle: It became itself a major participant in policy design, providing panache to the Enthoven ideas and leading other papers to pick up this hitherto esoteric plan. The *Times* editorials legitimized a particular policy approach to health care reform. Hacker quotes a Senate staffer saying that his senator told him he had to know more about this "because if the *New York Times* endorses it, then people are going to start talking about it."[3]

In the 1992 presidential campaign, candidate Clinton effectively used the need for health care reform as a club against President George Bush, without having to define any particular mode of reform. As president, he needed to change loose rhetoric into a concrete legislative proposal. Hilary Rodham Clinton, the first lady, headed a plan-writing team of literally hundreds of people, with an FOB (friend of Bill) smart in policy analysis but not politically sensitive, Ira Magaziner, as staff head. The exhaustive secret discussions came up with a liberal-conservative hybrid: managed competition with a fixed budget. The White House thought the Enthoven coterie would sign on for the competition and liberals for the fixed budget, which was how universal health coverage plans in other nations handled the problem of controlling costs. And cost control was by now the name of the game for all stakeholders, public and private, here and everywhere.

So a White House policy group, working with almost no contact with senators and congressmen, came up with a policy design—but, fatally, with only wishful thinking when it came to a *political* design. They apparently thought the diffuse support Clinton had received when espousing reform in vague campaign language would translate into grassroots pressure on Congress for whatever specific proposal the administration put forward. It didn't work out that way. Speaking of "health security" and "health alliances" without defining the terms turned out to be a poor substitute for the kind of local political organization that had carried the day for Democratic administrations in earlier times. The new looseness of party organization and every-candidate-for-himself electioneering for Congress deprived Clinton of the means by which to light a fire under the legislators. And his compromise seemed in the end to please neither right nor left by trying to combine elements from both.

Although the stakeholder interest groups (insurance companies, their associations, and the National Federation of Independent Business) were active and effective, one can read the defeat of Clinton's plan as much more the result of public relations failures and the nature of media reporting. Most of the reporting was by reporters whose beat was general politics, not health policy. They focused mostly on the political "game" and did little to help the public understand even the basics of a large and intricate tapestry of policy change. The administration's own public relations staff goofed by discouraging frank explanations of features that might be hard to explain—leaving all explanation to exactly those who would present every aspect in the worst possible light. The congressional campaign, on the other hand, depended on the policy details that the Clinton people thought could be used to create broad support in the political middle. In the end, the hybrid's details offended both liberals and conservatives, so there was no effective counterweight to all the political and institutional factors.

It may not be too great a stretch to say, leaning on Hacker's analysis, that the Clinton plan's failure was perhaps doomed less by interest group power and the particularities of congressional structure and process than by the attempt to fuse contradictory policy ideas into a political compromise that lacked internal conceptual integrity. Group power still exists, but its hold perhaps remains strongest on secondary matters; on truly major substance, ideas advanced by policy entrepreneurs from a variety of extrapolitical bases play a larger role.

In the immediate aftermath of what can only be described as a major political disaster, health care problems were relegated to the congressional back burner and off the general public's radar screen. Only a year later, however, an ironic twist was already becoming apparent. The political campaign urging people to keep government from getting into health care via the Clinton initiative had transmogrified into something of a national movement in the opposite direction, at least on some topics. Washington's attention had largely refocused on the Republican Contract with America and the 1996 presidential election, but the states had apparently been energized by all the publicity about health care problems. The surprising result was state government intrusion into the core of the doctor-patient relationship. By the end of 1996, the laws of 29 states specified that insurance must cover an inpatient stay of 48 hours for mother and newborn after a normal birth (96 hours for a Cesarean), and 3 other states achieved the same objective by voluntary agreements. Only 10 states rejected such bills (called "early discharge" legislation), and there were 7 outlier states in which early discharge bills had not been introduced. All this activity took place within 19 months of Maryland having taken the lead.

One careful study of the "drive-through delivery" legislative steamroller in the state legislatures did not find a civics book example of a deliberative process. Such a process is expected to include staff research, a variety of trial balloon bills being introduced over several years, extensive hearings, major floor debates, and a partisan vote reflecting philosophical principles or party ideology. Rather, clear evidence was lacking to favor either the new early discharge patterns or the older, longer-stay patterns.[4] So how did the boom in state laws get underway?

A complex of factors was involved. It was a "women's issue" par excellence, and state legislatures have an increasing number of female members, some of whom were instrumental in sponsoring early discharge bills. Physician organizations representing obstetricians and pediatricians were important stimulators, having good credibility on such an issue as defenders of their patients. Interestingly, testimony from the American College of Nursing Midwives stating that the crucial question was not how soon mother and newborn were sent home but whether the services available at home were adequate, was not responded to. (Two 1997 studies indicated that maternal inexperience was a bigger problem than early discharge, and follow-up home calls from a nurse might be a better and less costly way of helping new mothers and their children than a more extended hospital stay.)

One might have expected the antigovernment mood and Republican successes in the 1994 elections to work against such intrusive legislation. After all, the "drive-through delivery" bills amounted to both micromanagement and an unfunded mandate (a law requiring an organization to do something but not requiring the government to put up the money to support the action). Both were "no-nos" in the political lexicon of the late 1990s, but the positives for action were strong enough to overcome these obstacles, not least because no state funds were involved and insurance companies are an easy target. The media were delighted to play up the issue: It had emotional appeal, *seemed* to be non-technical and understandable, and played on rising concerns about HMOs, into which many of the middle class were being shifted by employers' coverage choices. It was a campaign driven by anecdotes and sound bites.

The political message was not lost on inside-the-Beltway politicians, and in September 1996 President Clinton signed a federal equivalent, the Newborns' and Mothers' Health Protection Act.

The public had become to a greater extent than usual an "attentive" public, and when the public—or at least its media surrogate—is attentive, political response of some kind is bipartisan. To the surprise of commentators and probably of legislators themselves, a near flood of health-related bills responded to the public's apparent concerns in 1996–1997. On the same day as the newborns' law, a bill was signed requiring that insurance policies extend to mental health the same coverage as medical-surgical needs. Later in the same month, a law was passed making it easier for employees to retain coverage when they change jobs, reacting to middle class fears of being downsized simultaneously out of both a job and health insurance.

The beat continued in the 105th Congress. The 1997 Balanced Budget Act included a $24 billion Children's Health Insurance Program intended to extend health insurance coverage to several million children, partly in response to a strange-bedfellow campaign that had been waged for months by Senator Orrin Hatch (R., Utah) and Edward Kennedy (D., Mass.). It also moved Medicare into offering more preventive measures: mammograms, Pap smears, screening for prostate and colon cancer and osteoporosis, and education for diabetics. And it broadened seniors' options by initiating a collection of new programs under the marketing label of Medicare + Choice. (See Chapter 5.) Congress had pushed through substantial changes.

By the end of 1997, it was clear that Congress had a split personality on the reach of government's health care role. It wanted to help ensure that those who had health coverage could receive care for whatever might be the medical condition *du jour* and was willing to extend coverage for some children. But it was not ready to ensure that all adults would have health coverage. And in 1998, the focus of congressional attention moved to the issues of patients' rights. Whatever the particular issue may be at a given moment or in a single session of Congress, the battle over government's role, as health financier for public sector programs and policy overseer for private sector health plans, will clearly continue to occupy Congress' attention in future years.

Meanwhile, President Clinton made it clear in 1997–1998 that he had no intention of being upstaged by the legislators. He seized upon the device of executive orders (which allow a president to fill in niches left out of legislation, so long as they do not contravene any laws) and used them extensively in a short period of time. Orders included the following:

- Guaranteeing to every person receiving health care through a federally sponsored program (Medicare, Medicaid, the armed services, the Indian Health Service, and federal employees) many of the patient rights recommended by the Advisory Commission on Consumer Protection and Quality. The guarantees include access to specialists and a right to appeal health plan decisions to an independent body. (February 1998)
- Providing some special protections to Medicare beneficiaries, especially those enrolled in HMOs, such as a right to information about the financial condition of health plans and how its physicians are paid, a woman's right to have direct access to gynecologists, applying a "prudent layperson's" rule to payment for ER visits, and prohibitions against HMO recruitment of subscribers in ways that purposely avoid the sick or the poor. (June 1998)
- Instituting special efforts to reach millions of children eligible for Medicaid but not enrolled. (June 1998)
- Ordering special outreach to inform some 4 million low-income Medicare beneficiaries that they have not availed themselves of a program to help pay their Part B premiums. (July 1998)
- Ordering that health plans be excluded from the large market of federal employees if the Office of Personnel Management finds that they are violating the letter or spirit of the Kassebaum-Kennedy law, which is intended to provide portability of benefits. (July 1998)
- Changing federal specifications for Medicaid eligibility to permit the inclusion of some 135,000–200,000 more people. (August 1998)

Executive orders (and lesser regulatory orders, emanating from the Department of Health and Human Services or its component Medicare agency, HCFA) are rarely challenged, because they can be posited as merely implementing the statutory will of Congress. The president seems to have a clear advantage in his competition with the legislature, for expressions of its desires that are not embedded in statutes that the president signs have no legal effect, but the president's executive orders constitute authoritative policy.

Although fundamental change is not part of the active agenda as this book goes to press, incremental change—the classic pattern in U.S. checks-and-balances politics—is so much in vogue that we should perhaps use an oxymoronic label—the Incremental Imperative—to characterize the current health policy scene. Although the president and Congress are unable or unwilling to accomplish radical reform, together and separately they were almost tripping over each other in the 1996–1998 period in their desire to show leadership in responding to the managed care backlash. Unfortunately, what they ended up showing was, once again, stalemate: insufficient agreement on what should be the extent of patients' rights to enact any law at all.

In many of the 50 states, however, the pressures to act have been more effective in the late 1990s, the early discharge laws described above being just one example. It's time to look more broadly at the states' involvement in health care issues in the 1990s.

Federalism Is Alive and Well in Health Care

One has to go back to the Progressive Era at the beginning of the century to find a period of activist state government as strong as that of the late 1990s. The New Deal (roughly, President Franklin D. Roosevelt's first two terms, 1933–1941) was this century's strongest period in the other direction. The apparent impotence of the states to see their citizens through a collapsed economy cried out for action from Washington, and FDR happily obliged. From then until President Ronald Reagan declared the national government to be the problem, not the solution, it was assumed by politicians and policy wonks that important problems required national action. Despite President Richard M. Nixon's call for a "new federalism" that would return power to the states, a public opinion survey in the early 1970s showed 70 percent favoring federal action to solve major problems, versus 63 percent favoring the states.

In 1998, however, a survey taken by the Pew Center for the People and the Press found that whereas 81 percent of respondents trusted the states to handle governmental problems, only 60 percent trusted the Feds.[5] Gary Wills says the states are "manifesting a new energy, almost a frenzy, in starting, altering or killing programs."[6] Charter schools, bilingualism in the schools, mandatory criminal sentences, welfare reform, term limits, and patient rights ranging from minimum stays for birthing to assisted suicide—all of these have seen far more action at the state than at the federal level. Being anti-Washington does not mean being antigovernment in the new state activism. And health care issues have been prominent items on the agenda.

Two major developments have been driving the states' involvement. One has been the ever-increasing cost of Medicaid during the past 20 years. Double-digit health care inflation produced an almost overwhelming burden on state treasuries. Part of this Medicaid cost increase, of course, was simply a sharing in overall health care inflation. But a large part was caused by growth in the clientele, a combined result of the recession and of congressional expansion of the eligibility for children and pregnant women. From both causes, annual state Medicaid expenditures grew nearly 17 percent in 1980 and stayed double-digit through 1993's increase of 13 percent. The situation got worse when state government incomes fell in the recession at the beginning of the 1990s. Only in the second half of the decade did the rate of increase decline substantially (to 3.8 percent in 1996), at least in part because many states were pushing their Medicaid populations into HMOs. (See Table 5.4 in Chapter 5.)

The second incentive for state activism in health care is political. The rapid, often involuntary switch of employees into managed care organizations, especially HMOs, was generally made with little realization of what the change portended. Living by a new set of organizational rules (clearance procedures for seeing a specialist, denials of treatments as experimental or simply outside the plan's scope of coverage, or denial of payment for an ER visit because the chest pain turned out to have been heartburn rather than a heart attack) and dealing with a medical bureaucracy rather than with a solo physician's office surprised, annoyed, and angered many enrollees. As anecdotes about HMO patients' problems began to receive a big play in the media—and that publicity itself seemed to generate more widespread unhappiness by leading patients to anticipate difficulties from their health plans—the inevitable next step was a demand that something be done.

Furthermore, the recession and the widely reported phenomenon of corporate downsizing (i.e., mass layoffs) produced large numbers of suddenly uninsured workers. When they found new jobs, many could not pick up new health insurance because of some chronic health problem that constituted a disqualifying preexisting condition. Middle managers, not just production workers, began to feel the stress of losing or fearing to lose coverage for themselves and their families, thus enlarging the pool of unhappy constituents. Governors and legislatures found that health was increasingly a politically salient subject. Positively, that made it a subject worth working on to please constituents; negatively, it became a pressure point that could not be ignored. Insurance companies have long been populist whipping boys, so the demands began to focus strongly on state legislators. And they could not pass the buck to Washington because it had been established since the 1940s, by the McCarran-Ferguson Act, that insurance regulation was almost entirely in the jurisdiction of the states.

In the absence of national action, one might have supposed a clear field for extensive state action to improve private insurance accessibility for their citizens, both for its own sake and to reduce the states' direct obligation for Medicaid patients. However, a catch-22 situation developed when the Employee Retirement Security Act (ERISA) of 1974 was judicially interpreted to prohibit state regulation of health benefits provided in a corporation's self-insured plan. (This means that the company uses its own funds as a health insurance claims account, perhaps hiring an insurance company only to administer the plan but not to be the insurer.) More than half of all companies with more than 50 employees do self-insure. With the federal government having largely abrogated any role in insurance regulation and ERISA foreclosing state action, the states have not been able to adopt health insurance market reforms that would apply evenhandedly to all health plans. For one thing, state legislatures have liked to mandate certain coverages in employer plans (e.g., chiropractic, dentistry, infertility treatments, or acupuncture in a number of states; heart transplants in Georgia; hairpieces in Minnesota; and marriage counseling in California), often at the behest of provider associations, but they cannot reach the self-insured ones.[7] This regulatory no man's land is much to the liking of employers, insurance companies, and managed care plans, who are essentially free to make whatever arrangements they like.

One recent bridge across the state-federal regulatory impasse was built when the Kassebaum-Kennedy bill to encourage portability of health insurance became law in 1996. It made an exception to ERISA so that self-insured plans are obligated to the same extent as regular insurance company plans.

But that's only one small step. When passing ERISA to protect workers, Congress enacted nationally uniform standards in the operation of pension plans. Accidentally, it resulted in denying compensation for lost wages, pain, and suffering as the law applies to modern managed care health plans. Even judges are frustrated by the apparent inequity of the vacuum thus created. A federal judge in Boston asserted in one case that it "is deeply troubling that, in the health insurance context, ERISA has evolved into a shield of immunity which thwarts the legitimate claims of the very people it was designed to protect."[8] At least two federal appeals courts have held that their hands are tied by the statute. So far there is no head of steam to accomplish change, partly because of opposition from health plans and their allies and partly because ERISA is a very complex statute.

The states' changes in Medicaid have been self-initiated to save tax moneys. States have manipulated the income eligibility threshold for adults (eligibility for children has been largely preempted by the federal government): The higher costs went, the lower the income level at which one became eligible for Medicaid. In many states, no adult is eligible whose income even approaches what Washington terms the poverty level. In the 1990s, the major thrust has been to create managed care systems for Medicaid enrollees.

But the states cannot accomplish this major switch unilaterally. Because Medicaid rests on national legislation and Washington pays more than half the total bill, the states are bound by regulations issued by HCFA, which administers both Medicaid and Medicare. Major changes must be approved via waivers from Washington, which often involve prolonged negotiations. In these negotiations the medically wise decision may not mesh with the politics of health care; administration political preferences in the nation's capitol often run contrary to gubernatorial calculations in the states.

Beyond Medicaid costs, state efforts to affect health care have focused on extending the financial availability of private health insurance through insurance reforms in the small group and individual policy markets; on boldly (in several cases) trying to achieve within their borders the universal coverage that has eluded national legislators; and, especially since the backlash against managed care reached a crescendo, on catering to demands for patients' rights of various kinds.

Literally thousands of bills have been thrown into state legislative hoppers to cover perceived health plan problems. To compare notes and pass reform ideas there has developed (with support from the Milbank Memorial Fund) a bipartisan association of officials and legislators from 40 states, called the Reforming States Group (RSG). It has worked with some members of Congress, including then-Senator Nancy Kassebaum when she was working on the portability bill with Senator Edward Kennedy. As 1997 ended, RSG was working with national and state legislators, executive branch officials, and multistate employers to develop a set of principles of health care federalism that state and federal policy makers might agree upon.[9]

Whether through bravery, bravura, or hubris, several states have tried to do what Congress and Clinton could not: achieve universal coverage for a state population. Massachusetts, Minnesota, Vermont, Washington, Florida, and Oregon all undertook efforts to expand coverage. It would be a good thing in itself, something politicians could reap electoral rewards for, and it would save money for the state by reducing the number who would need Medicaid assistance. Unfortunately, none of these worked as hoped. Some never got off the ground; some had to be pared down. The most interesting, because it involves a unique and still-controversial approach to Medicaid, is Oregon's—the Oregon plan for rationing, as it became known. Not only was the plan unique, but its originator and later implementer was a physician—state legislator, president of the state Senate, and later governor, Dr. John Kitzhaber.

Medicaid's conventional mode of operation is to set eligibility rules by categories (e.g., mothers with dependent children, pregnant women, children up to a statutorily fixed age, and income at some percentage of the federal poverty level). For eligible persons, the scope of coverage is essentially the same as in an average private plan.

In Oregon, funding for bone marrow transplants in the Medicaid program (which had begun on a case-by-case basis in 1985) was deleted in a competition in 1987 among special social programs that the legislature felt it could not wholly fund. The deletion became a political issue when a Medicaid mother's young boy died in the midst of a widely publicized effort to raise private funds to pay for his operation.

Kitzhaber, in a Legislative Emergency Board subcommittee meeting to discuss a special appropriation of $200,000 to fund five bone marrow transplant requests, alerted the body to a more basic issue: He argued that with 450,000 Oregonians lacking *any* health coverage, there would be a basic inequity because many Oregonians' taxes would be used "to buy services for people on public assistance that they can not even get for their own children."[10] The subcommittee voted against the funding. That night, on his *Nightline* television show, Ted Koppel raised the political stakes for the full Emergency Board meeting the next day when he said that Oregon had "allowed this boy to die" when it stopped funding organ transplants. Kitzhaber picked up the challenge, stating during the board meeting that "we are going to have to ration health care."[11]

Then began a five-year effort to design and legislate a radical change. Federal-state complexities, political more than technical, tied the plan up until the necessary waiver was approved in March 1993; the plan became effective in February 1994. Oregon became the first state to ensure health coverage for all its citizens below the poverty line (and in the process greatly simplified operations by eliminating all eligibility categories except family income) and did so by spelling out a list of prioritized medical conditions and treatments. The priority list that emerged after extended and repeated trial runs and public meetings is priced out (i.e., an estimate is made of the annual cost of each item on the list) and a line is drawn annually at the point where the treatments to be included exactly matches the legislative appropriation for the forthcoming year. In 1995, the list contained 744 items, but the appropriation level necessitated covering none below priority number 581.

As enacted, the Oregon plan covered 114,000 previously uninsured people. A great success as far as it goes. The original intent, however, had also been to cover a group of high-risk people with uninsurable conditions and to use an employer mandate to provide coverage for working families whose income was above poverty but who had no access to private health insurance. The mandate was later rescinded, so some 400,000 Oregonians remain uninsured. In this respect, the Oregon case resembles efforts in several other states to achieve universal coverage within their borders: "expectations far exceeding accomplishments," as Howard M. Leichter has written.[12]

Yet the states are clearly among the crucial players in health care policy today. Many of them have undertaken health insurance market reforms to improve access for employees of small businesses and their employers, to guarantee portability for persons changing jobs, to eliminate preexisting condition clauses, and to change other insurance practices that constitute obstacles to obtaining coverage. Oregon has been bolder than any other state and may well have been paving the road to the entire nation's future by employing the strategy of a basic benefits package to ensure that poverty alone does not make one uninsurable. The role of the states as experimental laboratories for the nation remains vibrant. The ultimate limit on that role (as we saw in Chapter 2 regarding the failure of the Kerr-Mills Act) is that a policy that one wants to have apply to the whole nation requires action by the whole nation.

The Cast of Characters and Their Strategies

Each area of policy making has a largely identifiable list of players and a set of at least partly structured relationships. It's time to look at the actors in health policy and how they go about affecting what government does.

Governmental Players

Money has been called the mother's milk of politics; it is also the determining factor in congressional committee jurisdiction whenever changes in the health entitlement programs, Medicare and Medicaid, are being considered. House Ways and Means and Senate Finance are the most basic committees, because their taxing authority includes approving the substantive programs for which money is to be raised. (Once a program has been authorized, the appropriations committee in each house becomes the crucial player.) Congress also has policy committees that develop expertise in particular functional areas. For health, the most important generally are Senate Labor and Human Resources and House Energy and Commerce, whose Health and Environment subcommittee has had independent importance. The Clinton health plan was also considered by the House Education and Labor Committee, so these were the five major venues for lobbying and entrepreneurial jockeying by legislators. On such a major bill every committee chair wanted a prominent piece of the action. A "giant spitting contest," as one staff aide termed it, took place between Senator Daniel Patrick Moynihan (D., N.Y.), who chaired Senate Finance and claimed the bill because revenue measures, plus Medicare and Medicaid, were part of that committee's normal jurisdiction, and Edward M. Kennedy, Labor and Human Resources chair, who had been UHI's main legislative champion for a quarter-century.

Several staff agencies adjunct to the Congress have become important players in health policy. One is the General Accounting Office (GAO), which began in 1921 as a watchdog against malfeasance or simple inefficiency in spending the taxpayers' dollars. In recent decades it has developed a program evaluation staff of analysts, in addition to its accountants. Its reports on agency operations often stimulate (and are to some extent a surrogate for) serious congressional oversight and occasionally provide materials that become significant factors in policy debate. A 1991 GAO study estimated that moving to a single payer system like Canada's, in which government was the only player and insurance company marketing and overhead expenses would be eliminated, would reduce costs by 20 percent. In 1993–1994, this gave ammunition to the Democratic faction urging a single-payer plan as an alternative to Clinton's complicated managed competition approach. In the first half of the 1990s, the GAO turned out over 20 reports dealing with health care reform.

The Congressional Budget Office (CBO) has also acquired a significant role by producing nonpartisan, highly respected estimates of the costs of any proposed piece of legislation. Sometimes its figures help the Democrats, sometimes the Republicans. In "scoring" the Clinton plan, the CBO said it would add $75 billion to health costs, severely damaging the administration's claim that it would save $60 billion.[13] Even more devastating for Clinton's side, the CBO—despite much arm-twisting and a telephonic dressing down of its director, Robert Reischauer, by Senator Kennedy[14]—declared the payments to be made into the Health Security system by employers and employees to be taxes, not private premiums.

Two staff bodies were created in the 1980s to assist Congress in monitoring new Medicare payment systems intended to control hospital and physician costs. Begun as semitechnical organizations with staffs expert in economics and medical management, both the Prospective Payment Assessment Commission (ProPAC) (overseeing hospitals) and the Physician Payment Review Commission (PPRC) (overseeing physicians) have issued annual reports that provide broad reviews of such matters as national health spending trends, developments in Medicare's managed care plans, the quality of care, consumer protections, and the financing of graduate medical education. (In 1997, ProPAC and PPRC were merged into a single commission, the Medicare Payment Advisory Committee, or MedPAC.) Commission recommendations are often followed by Congress, so the commissions have been able to attract very capable persons from health care administration and academia into their membership. In so doing, they constitute a quasi-corporatist element in American government: a kind of joint decision making between government officials and major group interests, in which the groups are actually part of the governmental body rather than a supplicant to it. This pattern has been strongly developed in Germany and Japan, but is unusual in the United States.

Turning to the executive branch, the obvious place to start is the Department of Health and Human Services (DHHS). Several of its units are major health care players. Prominent components include the Health Care Financing Administration (HCFA) that operates Medicare and Medicaid, the Food and Drug Administration (FDA), the Indian Health Service, the National Institutes of Health (NIH), and the Centers for Disease Control (CDC). NIH is organized largely by disease (e.g., National Heart Institute, National Cancer Institute, National Institute of Diabetes and Digestive and Kidney Diseases)—an arrangement purposefully designed to make it easier to build political support for medical research by personalizing it. The newest of the DHHS health units is the Agency for Health Care Policy and Research (AHCPR). It has an increasingly significant role as a catalyst for the development of guidelines regarding the most effective treatments for many medical conditions.

Military medical care is an oft-forgotten but financially significant part of the federal government's health budget. Health programs for active duty and retired armed forces personnel cost $13.4 billion in 1996, and the Department of Veterans Affairs medical expenditure was even larger: $16.7 billion. (And that's not counting Medicare benefits for over-65 veterans.) Organizations like the American Legion and Veterans of Foreign Wars are zealous advocates for their constituencies, one result being that it seems to be harder to close a VA hospital than an active duty military base. With all World War II veterans

Medicare eligible, integration of their care with that of nonveterans of the same age makes a lot of sense for the bulk of health care needs, but such a change represents a political minefield. What makes medical and economic sense does not always work politically; in other words, it may not generate enough support among legislators beset by interest group pressures within their districts or states.

Broadest in its reach is the Office of Management and Budget (OMB) in the Executive Office of the president. Originated as the Bureau of the Budget in 1921, its original purpose was defined by its first head in this way:

> Much as we love the President, if Congress, in its omnipotence over appropria-
> tions and in accordance with its authority over policy, passed a law that garbage
> should be put on the White House steps, it would be our regrettable duty, as a bu-
> reau, in an impartial, nonpolitical, and non-partisan way to advise the Executive
> and Congress as to how the largest amount of garbage could be spread in the most
> expeditious and economical manner.[15]

At least since World War II, this essential presidential staff arm has become an evaluator of what to do as well as of how, because effective government depends on how well designed a program is to reach its objective, not just on how cost-efficiently it is operated. So OMB is a player when presidential decisions are made about such health care decisions as whether to create strong incentives for Medicare enrollees to join HMOs, or which of several competing proposals the president should support to ensure health coverage for a higher percentage of children.

Nonprofits and Private Sector Players

A very strong part of the mix consists of nonprofit organizations. Some are disease specific, like the American Diabetes Association, the National Multiple Sclerosis Society, and the Alzheimers Association. In such cases, nonprofit does not mean financially disinterested; a major purpose of many such organizations is to lobby for increased funding for whatever health function or treatment approach or clientele group it is organized around.

Sometimes the effort to attract legislators' attention takes novel forms: The American Heart Association delivered synthetic brains to all senators and members of the House of Representatives in 1998—not to slam their intelligence but to inform them about the danger of strokes, which kill 160,000 people a year. A recent survey of legislators and staffers revealed that only 4 percent of them were aware that stroke is the third largest killer of Americans.[16]

Now they can be reminded daily by viewing a blob in a jar of purple liquid on their desks.

Also important are a small number of charitable foundations (e.g., Kaiser Family Foundation, the Robert Wood Johnson Foundation) that are instrumental in funding demonstration projects of new treatment modalities and institutional patterns of care and in evaluating health policy developments.

A listing of professional associations relevant to health care reform of course begins with the American Medical Association (AMA). At one time, it could almost have been said to have ended there, too, for its spokespersons were once assumed to speak for all medical professionals. After its long-standing opposition to government financing of health care for any but the very poor failed to stop Congress from passing Medicare, its day of singular influence waned. A major public relations gaffe occurred in 1997 when its administrative leadership contracted with a home care appliance company, Sunbeam Corporation, to allow the firm to use the AMA logo on its health products (such as blood pressure monitors, vaporizers, and heating pads) in exchange for royalties on gross sales. Criticism exploded, with its members as well as with the general public. It canceled the deal (but had to pay Sunbeam several million dollars in compensation for voiding the contract), and the executive vice president resigned.

With its membership down from 82 percent of physicians in 1962 to 43 percent in 1998, the AMA has lost some of its claim to be the "voice" of the medical profession. (Its leaders might wish to emulate Germany, where physicians are required to join the medical association of their region, which are then in a strong negotiating position.) Furthermore, only 34 percent of doctors under 40 are members, and the AMA now has to share the spotlight with 115 specialist societies, some of which maintain their own Washington lobbying offices. The head of the New York Medical Society's young physician section has said that "We're dealing with a different breed of physician from the generation that preceded us. They're increasingly in debt, have different practice patterns, and more and more of them are employed. The medical societies were slow to recognize these demographic shifts." AMA data show that 42 percent of direct-care physicians are now employed by HMOs, hospitals, medical groups, or government agencies.[17]

A similar situation exists on the hospital side. The American Hospital Association is not a "one size covers all" organization. Its sometimes allies–sometimes competitors in politicking include the Federation of American Health Systems (for-profit hospitals), the Catholic Health Association, the Council of Teaching Hospitals, and the National Council of Community Hospitals.

Then there are the American Nurses Association, the Blue Cross and Blue Shield Association, the Joint Commission on Accreditation of Health Care Organizations, the National Committee for Quality Assurance (NCQA), the Group Health Association of America/American Managed Care and Review Association, and the American Health Care Association, the last two being trade groups of HMOs and for-profit nursing homes. Both professional and trade associations have the economic interests of their dues-paying members as a major reason for being—and therefore for politicking—although associations of professionals are presumed still to acknowledge an obligation to the community as a whole. Given the trillion-dollar stakes, the ongoing corporatization and business consolidation of health care is not surprising—only its rapid pace is. For example, Columbia/HCA owned 340 hospitals at its peak, many of them converted from community nonprofit status. Another for-profit chain, Tenet Healthcare Corporation, owns 130. The majority of HMOs are now profit-seeking firms as well, and a continuous integration through mergers is taking place.

The practice of medicine itself is undergoing this kind of business integration as solo practitioners and whole physician groups are being bought by physician management organizations, a few of which are publicly owned national corporations. And some specialist groups are combining in order to win contracts with HMOs. American Oncology Resources, for example, has been buying up the practices of oncologists, and as of summer 1997 this management practice business represented 256 specialists in 15 states.[18] As the varied subindustry segments of health care grow into national business entities, the national political stakes for, and the clout of, such firms increase.

Business corporations stand front and center on the health care stage in two ways. Because the preponderance of private health coverage (over 85 percent) is through corporate employee benefit plans, business firms have a direct stake in health policy. Some large manufacturing companies overcame (at least in the early stages) their traditional distaste for all government programs and supported the Clinton plan in 1994 because it would require smaller competitors to provide employee coverage. This requirement would make it harder for the smaller firms to underbid larger rivals who have long paid substantial sums for union-negotiated health plans. And of course many, many companies belong to organizations with generalized pro-business interests, such as the National Association of Manufacturers, the Chamber of Commerce, and (for the blue chips) the Business Roundtable.

For smaller businesses, the National Federation of Independent Business (NFIB) has become a major political protagonist, in part because of its leadership in fighting the employer mandate aspect of the Clinton plan. It was immediately and unalterably opposed to any law that would compel employers to fund health care or even to share its funding with employees, and it used both direct and grassroots lobbying in a very aggressive manner. At a time when the Clinton administration had four people working the House of Representatives, NFIB had six. It sent over 2 million pieces of mail to small business owners with information for them to use when visiting legislators in their district offices, it developed public forums to turn out impressive numbers of business people opposed to the Clinton plan, and it did innumerable media interviews.

Similar operations were mounted by the Health Insurance Association of America (HIAA), which raised $30 million beyond its normal budget. The huge war chest—and that term well fits the tenor of the health care campaigns of 1993–1994—enabled HIAA to hire field organizers, to send nearly half a million pieces of mail (both snailmail and E-mail), and to make phone and personal visit contacts with senators and representatives. And the personal visits were from hometown people, not impersonal Beltway-based lobbyists. Making "businesses look like populists" had become an established industry in the nation's capital, and in the view of two thoughtful journalists, Haynes Johnson and David S. Broder, business success in fighting off a larger government role in health care in 1994 is but one instance of a larger theme: "When business and its allies line up against organized labor, consumer groups, and other liberal organizations . . . the latter are almost always out-organized, out-spent, outgunned."[19]

This phenomenon is not exactly news. It has been a political science truism for more than a half-century that although group power may be pluralistic, it is far from evenly distributed. At the same time, it would be unnecessarily cynical to assert that the big money and the major interests always pull ahead at the finish line. The AMA lost the Medicare battle in 1965; the NFIB and its business partners lost in 1993 when Congress passed President Clinton's Family and Medical Leave Act; and hospitals lost in 1996 when drive-through delivery limits were mandated.

Less publicized than the actions of Fortune 500 companies and peak associations are the efforts of provider groups (e.g., osteopaths, chiropractors, acupuncturists), pharmaceutical firms, and medical device manufacturers to turn public policies and programs to their economic advantage. On narrower issues, particular organizations and firms may be quite effective.

PSA, the test for prostate cancer, provides a good example of successful campaigning for a specific procedure. It remains controversial nearly 15 years after approval by FDA for checking the progress of cancers already diagnosed. It is now recommended by the American Cancer Society and the American Urological Society as a screening test for all men over age 50, but it has not been endorsed for that purpose by the United States Preventive Services Task Force. Despite the lack of consensus, PSA is very widely used. The test is a simple office procedure, but 20 percent of the tests show cancer where there is none (false positives) and one-fourth of men with prostate cancer have normal test levels.[20]

So why has demand for it become what one urologist called an "avalanche"? A marketing campaign that began with a Prostate Cancer Awareness Week in 1989. The week is paid for by makers of the test and of treatment medications, and the American Cancer Society has been a cosponsor. When it began, the campaign drew 15,000 men to testing centers. By 1993, half a million tests a year were being done.[21] In 1997, the American College of Physicians published update information and a set of guidelines stating pros and cons of testing and treatment and ending with the advice that "routine PSA measurement without a frank discussion of the issues is inappropriate."[22]

The largest of all organizations having a strong interest in health care is the American Association of Retired Persons (AARP). With approximately 35 million members (a sizable fraction of whom are in their fifties and not retired), it is the politically dominant voice of Medicare beneficiaries. It is also a large business enterprise, selling health (and other) insurance policies and other services and publishing a bimonthly magazine, *Modern Maturity,* that has a larger circulation than *TV Guide.*

Political action committees (PACs), the 800-pound gorillas of campaign finance, may be called an offshoot of grassroots lobbying: They are a way of having an organization funnel contributions from a substantial number of people to a candidate's campaign coffers. Major health-related legislation has been a focal point, and the money has come not only from insurance and pharmaceutical corporations but also from AMPAC (the PAC of the AMA), the American Dental Association, Blue Shield, hospital and nursing groups, and manufacturers of medical devices. The more than 200 health-related PACs may sometimes cancel one another out, and there is little hard data on specific accomplishments; however, they are clearly major players in the legislative game.

Critics charge that substantial contributions often produce votes favoring the contributing group's position, but correlation is not cause and proven bribery instances are rare in modern national politics. Much PAC money is spent to support those legislators known to favor a group's position, as a kind of "thank you" or insurance policy. Some is spent attempting to neutralize potential opponents. And all is spent as a way of gaining "access"—easy entree to the legislator's office to present one's views. One hears few cries of outrage when people charged with buying votes respond with, "Not at all. I'm just gaining access." It follows that our current political ethic accepts allowing money to make some voters "more equal than others" in this manner. (Should it? I ask the reader.)

Although many of the organizations named in these paragraphs have power and influence in their own right, even the largest like to partner (a word that has interestingly acquired a verb form as the forging of coalitions becomes a common feature of the American politico-economic scene). Partnering is partly a function of the sheer proliferation of organized groups in recent decades and partly of the replacement of "iron triangles" by the looser alliances called "issue networks." In the more open politics of post-Watergate investigative media coverage and looser party affiliations among the entrepreneurial legislators, broad coalitions are more the pattern. Grassroots politicking to shape public opinion via mass media efforts is more notable on the larger issues than buttonholing legislators in the hallways of the Capitol. It is partly a matter of financial efficiency, sharing the cost of large campaigns directed at a joint target, and partly of creating strength by the appearance of representing a very broad spectrum of constituencies. These issue networks are different in another way, too. Unlike the traditional pressure group pattern, they involve technical and professional experts, often academics, in the partnering, thus reflecting the intellectually more sophisticated nature of the issues and the politicking today. Sheer numbers of members won't do it any more; the best substantive arguments become more important as the scientific–social scientific as well as physical–biological scientific content of public policy issues intensifies.

The phrase technical complexity may bring to mind things like nuclear nonproliferation treaties. Equally complex, however, and more difficult to deal with because not quantifiable, are human behavior topics like welfare reform and how to reduce drug use—and, of course, the myriad of changes that President and Mrs. Clinton and her 500-person social invention team tried to encompass in one big health care reform bill.

Abortion Stakeholders and the Courts

Not all stakeholding is financial in motivation. Some consists of public policy advocacy by groups seeking broad changes that they believe will benefit large segments of the population, rather than primarily themselves. Physicians for a National Health Program has been a major proselytizing group for a Canadian kind of system; the Heritage Foundation, a libertarian-oriented think tank, has argued for a more privatized health care system.

Ours has been called a more litigious society than most, so it is not surprising that group advocacy sometimes takes the form of lawsuits as well as legislative lobbying. The civil rights movement, with Thurgood Marshall as legal strategist for the National Association for the Advancement of Colored People (NAACP) some years before he became a Supreme Court justice, made very effective use of a series of carefully calibrated court cases in the 1940s and 1950s to break down legal segregation that kept black Americans out of law schools and colleges in the South. Those cases paved the way for *Brown v. Board of Education* in 1954, reversing the unrealistic "separate but equal" doctrine enunciated in *Plessy v. Ferguson* in 1896.

In health care, too, Supreme Court decisions have sometimes played an important role. The most notable instance is *Roe v. Wade,* the 1973 decision articulating a constitutional right to privacy and applying it to a woman's decision about having an abortion. That seemingly final verdict has turned out to be only the opening round of a continuing political and legal dispute. The Court's decision divided pregnancy into trimesters and said the states might still regulate the procedure "in ways reasonably related to maternal health" during the second trimester, and even prohibit abortions in the third trimester except to preserve the "life or health of the mother." Since 1973, therefore, Americans have had a national policy constitutionally based in both the supremacy clause and the doctrine of judicial review, yet with room for the states to continue political maneuvering about the conditions under which this right would be exercised. Many states took advantage of the opening and a round of legislated regulations followed by legal challenges to them ensued.[23]

In 1989, 16 years after *Roe,* the Supreme Court came one vote away from reversing itself when it decided a case involving Missouri's restrictions on abortion, including a requirement that the doctor do tests to tell if the fetus was "viable." If it was, the doctor could not do the abortion. In *Webster v. Reproductive Health Services,* the Court upheld the state's rules, and four justices were apparently ready to overturn *Roe* in the process. Justice Sandra Day O'Connor angered that group by casting her vote on the basis that Missouri had not placed an "undue burden" on the pregnant woman, so the decision could favor the state regulations but stay within the earlier decision.

Technology also entered the picture: The tests for viability undermined the factual logic of the original decision. Division of pregnancy into three equal segments was convenient for the justices, but medical advances had made that division untenable, as fetuses could be delivered alive much earlier than had been the case in 1973. Since *Webster,* the battle continues, in Congress and in the states. Each year in funding Medicaid, Congress enacts wording restricting or forbidding the use of public funds to pay for abortions, making it a procedure with a reverse means test: You can have an abortion if you have the money to pay for it yourself.

Abortion politics and civil rights have a similarity beyond judicial involvement to decide issues too hot for normal politics. Both of these areas of substantive public policy have had (and are still having) consequences for the political parties and electoral politics. Civil rights deeply divided the Democratic Party (causing the 1948 Dixiecrat revolt against President Harry S. Truman) and abortion policies currently are causing a deep fissure in the Republican Party. Platform fights at national Republican conventions in the 1990s are one of the surface manifestations.

These political consequences of policy decisions illustrate a fundamental point about politics and policy. Political scientists have long studied and written of the myriad ways in which the politics of groups and parties affect public policy. For example, differences between the major parties over the role of government have so far prevented the enactment of any national health insurance system that would guarantee coverage for all citizens. Yet these parties have permitted passage of Medicare and Medicaid to provide coverage for those identified as special cases: the elderly and some of the poor. The reciprocal impact of the substance of policy upon parties and the political process has only been studied extensively—and given a recognized place in the curriculum—in the past 25 years. Another example of such reciprocity is provided by the Kassebaum-Kennedy law of 1997, in which the perceived policy need of the middle class for health coverage produced a cross-party alliance to impose obligations on insurers and employers to give employees continuity of coverage when changing jobs. The connection between policy substance and the political process is very much a two-way street.

The Ultimate Stakeholders: The Patients

Health care politics is group politics, lobbying politics, opinion manipulation politics, and financial politics. In other words, it is part of the American political mainstream. Its specific differences from other domestic politics issues center on two facts: (1) It is the biggest industry in the land: $1 trillion "and change," as the saying goes, and 9.7 million employees in mid-1997 (a very substantial increase from 7.8 million just five years earlier)[24] and, (2) its subject matter is literally of life and death significance to all Americans.

If we define stakeholders as those having a vital interest in an area of decision making, then the patients are the ultimate stakeholders of the health care system. As with the general public in other areas, however, the patients are also the least organized. The well-organized and well-financed producers (providers, in health care) are the only generally recognized stakeholders. Health care conferences focus much more sharply on the needs of those who make a living out of health care—hospitals, medical device manufacturers, physician groups, managed care plans, all the allied health professions associations, and the hundreds of ancillary corporations and associations—than on those whose health status is crucially dependent on the "health care delivery system."

As patients-consumers, individual Americans are not even the purchasers of the health care "product." An employer or a government agency does most of the health care purchasing, whereas the individual's role is that of "copayer." Health care accountability runs mostly to the institutional purchasers, not in any direct sense to patients. No wonder there is public concern and calls are heard for a patient bill of rights and for ombudspersons when the recognized stakeholders are increasingly giants and wannabe giants of the corporate world.

But mandating patients' rights may not do the job by itself. Marc A. Rodman, an attorney and health policy specialist, argues that legislative oversight needs "a powerful consumer movement" to make it effective. He points out that organized advocacy about disabilities and specific diseases (e.g., AIDS, breast cancer, and polio) has been effective and shows what can be done. But advocacy organization needs to be broadened to cover all facets of consumers' relationships with managed care, he asserts, if health consumers are to end their competitive disadvantage in facing the medical producers.[25]

The basic question about future health care debates is this: Will they be driven primarily by group clout and sophisticated "marketing" through opinion-forming television commercials, or will they be informed by feedback from an electorate that has been presented with substantive debate and values clarification from their political leadership and that has its own advocacy organizations?

4

Beneath the Dilemmas, the Trilemma

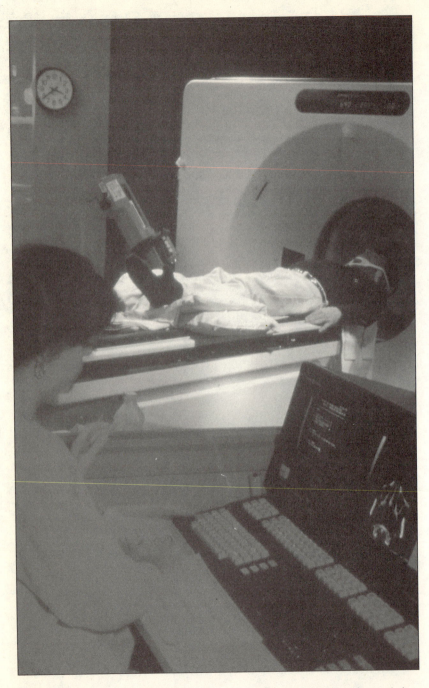

CAT scanner. Photo courtesy of Popperfoto/Archive Photos, reprinted with permission.

W HAT WOULD THE "PERFECT" (in quotation marks, for *no* system is ever perfect) health care system look like? It would have three dimensions:

1. Highest quality of care.
2. Maximum access.
3. Lowest cost.

Is there a problem here? Yes. Optimizing any two of these usually undermines the third. Which means we have to make choices, some of which are necessarily unhappy. In economic terms, that's called facing the opportunity costs: Doing A and B sometimes means giving up an opportunity to do C. Maximizing quality and access makes it impossible to minimize costs, and so on. So we have not just a dilemma, but a *trilemma*. Before seeing why that is so, we need to examine some of the questions and complexities within each of these goals.

How Do We Define Quality Care?

High quality in medical care is popularly exemplified by things like a startling new kind of brain surgery, or our ability to keep alive ever-smaller infants (some with birthweights less than a pound), or a breakthrough antibiotic. Americans read about teams of 10 or 15 physicians, nurses, and various technicians working together to perform a single procedure in the operating room (OR). They see medical miracles accomplished on television, in both dramas and documentaries. And Americans all take vicarious pride in these wonders, citing them to claim world superiority in health care.

But there are perspectives on quality beyond the gee-whiz of technology. One is how much "bang for the buck" Americans get versus what people in other nations get. Infant mortality (defined as deaths under one year per thousand live births) and life expectancy (at birth) are commonly accepted as markers of health system functioning. How does the United States stack up? Table 4.1 gives

TABLE 4.1   Health Status Indicators, 1995

		Life Expectancy	
	Infant Mortality	*Men*	*Women*
U.S.	8.0	72.5	79.2
Canada	6.0	75.3	81.3
United Kingdom	6.0	74.3	79.7
Germany	5.3	73.0	79.5
Japan	4.3	76.4	82.8

Source: OECD Health Data 97. OECD, Paris, 1997.

Note: U.S. infant mortality 7.2 in 1997. (Source: DHHS press release, October 7, 1998)

the numbers. Note that the lowest figure is the desirable one for infant mortality, while the highest number is, of course, what we want for life expectancy.

Are you surprised? Most Americans are, perhaps because they just assume that they have the best health care and would naturally have the strongest data. At least for these two basic parameters, Americans have a noticeable lag. With one exception: U.S. life expectancy at age 80 ranks number one.[1] Why would that be so? Perhaps because the United States has a higher rate than other nations of usage of technology for those of advanced age, and that is when such interventions may be most meaningful.

Another startling fact is that hospitals are dangerous to your health. A June 1998 Department of Health and Human Services report on the challenge of assuring high quality in the next century cited as a major problem the 180,000 hospital deaths that occur each year because of preventable errors.

As health plans compete for employer contracts and employers try to please employees, medical outcomes and patient satisfaction are two of the most discussed indicators of quality. Has the medical problem been solved, the disease cured? That's the biomedical question. How happy is the patient with her treatment, her providers, and her health plan? That's the bedside manner question. Both of these concerns are relative newcomers to health care discussions. They have come to the fore as a consequence of the rising insistence of those who pay for most care—private employers and government agencies—that they get the most for their money. Being able to compare competing plans and knowing what your employees do and don't like are now vital parts of the system.

Why have they not always been so important? Partly because when medical care could do less and did not consume such a large chunk of gross domestic product (GDP), there was simply less of a publicly noticeable problem. A second reason lies in the basic organization of health care. Medical practice is moving rapidly from a world of individual practitioners hanging out their shingles after finishing medical school and a year of internship to one of large groups of physicians, chains of hospitals, and corporate health plans. Add a third factor of computerized record keeping and the invention of data-gathering systems, the most widely used being the Health Plan Employer Data and Information Set (HEDIS) devised by the National Committee for Quality Assurance (NCQA), a nonprofit organization. Now there are the technical means and organizational setting in which to *begin* to measure outcomes and assess medical quality. As such capabilities are refined, the results can be used internally for quality control programs and externally by employers in selecting health plans.

NCQA has developed an accreditation program for managed care plans, and, as of fall 1997, it was able to release information on over 300 plans covering 37 million people.[2] What did it find? Its president, Margaret E. O'Kane, said that the range of health plan performance was "striking" and used heart attack treatment for an example. Many studies have shown the effectiveness of beta blockers in saving patients' lives, but only 30 percent of heart attack patients in some plans received them, whereas 90 percent did in some other plans. "Patients lost in the gap between what is achievable and what we actually achieve," she said, "are at greatly increased risk for another heart attack, and even death." A similar range was found in childhood immunizations: 81 percent of children under age two in New England received appropriate immunizations, but only 59 percent did in the Rocky Mountain region.

To put it simply, NCQA data show that health care quality in America is sometimes excellent, sometimes quite poor. It would clearly benefit employer-payers and their employee-enrollees to look at such data when comparing plans under consideration. But do findings about quality matter when contracts are being let for employee health coverage? Not enough. Although increasing, the proportion of use is relatively slight so far. Only one-third of companies with 200 or more workers were familiar with Health Plan Employer Data and Information Set (HEDIS) data (which provide the best available statistics) in one 1997 survey. Another poll of employers reported 60 percent as being "very concerned" about quality—but less so than about government regulation and rising premiums.[3]

Two other organizations are developing quality measurement systems. One is the Foundation for Accountability (FACCT), a consortium of health care plan purchasers. It has developed quality indicators for asthma, diabetes, depression, and breast cancer, and is working on more topics. Another is AHCPR's Consumer Assessment of Health Plans, which is cooperating with NCQA on a survey to measure patient assessments of their health care experiences. To assist Medicare patients, HCFA is cooperating with several of the private sector efforts; for example, it is funding a study to analyze issues of implementing FACCT's measures and to set up several pilot projects. As more seniors join managed care plans, these efforts become increasingly important.[4]

Seeking to simplify this competing plethora of quality-indicator programs, and presumably also to strengthen his credentials as the health policy presidential candidate for the year 2000, Vice President Al Gore announced in June 1998 the formation of a quality forum to ensure that consumers would have a consistent set of standards for helping them choose health plans on a quality basis.[5] The idea is to develop a consensus on common standards and guidelines that will make for more cost-effective health care.

Simplicity is clearly to be desired: To meet the demands of employer-purchasers, enrollees, and government agencies, one health plan reportedly had to file nine different reports with 675 different items of information.

We should note one other aspect of quality-measuring organizations: They all become players urging public policy makers to encourage or regulate health care in particular directions. The group-interest landscape of health care is continually enlarging.

Patient satisfaction is now offered as an alternative litmus test to medical outcomes—at least by managed care companies whose patient surveys show high approval ratings. Although one surely wants patients to be happy with their treatment, the problem with happy-camper surveys is that their claims of quality amount to such evidence as the phone is answered promptly, or the doctor the enrollee has known for 20 years is on the approved panel, or health club services are offered. When Oxford Health Plan advertised that it was "No. 1 in customer satisfaction," we learned nothing about how much their enrollees' medical conditions had improved. Although not to be discounted, customer satisfaction is tangential to the heart of medical care: clinical outcomes of treatment. Furthermore, the "report cards" currently becoming fashionable may lend themselves excessively to gaming: asking only the questions that are likely to produce the highest satisfaction scores. As quality analyst Donald M. Berwick has said, improving scores is not necessarily the same as improving care.[6] For example, raising a plan's screening mammography rate is not as important as improving the diagnosis and treatment patterns of cancer patient care; the latter is what truly measures quality. If report cards are less than 100 percent useful documents to aid individual (or employer-purchaser) choices among health plans, it may be of some ironic value that Americans pay little attention to ratings, even when done by independent experts. Friends and family views are more attended to.[7]

So what really defines quality: Satisfied patients? Processes that are generally thought to produce good results? Hospital staff-to-patient nursing ratios that meet American Nurses Association standards? How about having the lowest rate of deaths for a heart bypass operation among the hospitals in a given area? It may prove excellence of care, or it may prove that the heart team at that hospital avoids the most problematic cases. Measuring quality is much more difficult than one might suppose. Even defining it is hard, so it may be useful to have at hand the definition offered by the top-drawer National Institutes of Medicine: "the degree to which health services for individuals and populations increase the likelihood of desired health outcomes and are consistent with current professional knowledge."[8]

What distinguishes good from poor quality? A RAND report sponsored by the National Coalition on Health Care offers these guidelines:

Good quality means providing patients with appropriate services in a technically competent manner, with good communication, shared decision making, and cultural sensitivity. In practical terms, poor quality can mean *too much care* (e.g., unnecessary tests, medications, and procedures, with associated risk and side effects), *too little care* (e.g., not receiving a lifesaving surgical procedure), or the *wrong care* (e.g., medicines that should not be given together, poor surgical technique).[9]

Whether the meaning of quality is defined as medical outcomes or consumer satisfaction will depend in large part on what the payers see as most important to them. That means partly which plan their workers like best, but also which plan keeps employees healthy enough to minimize sick days and lost productivity. As quality measurement improves and becomes more widely known to employers and employees, one hopes that health plans will have to pay close attention—that competition will move more toward quality than price as the most vital factor.

We should perhaps not be too hard on the private employers purchasing health care. After nearly a decade of searching for the holy grail of hard numbers that will empirically prove one plan to have better outcomes than another, the questing individuals and organizations seem to see their target receding almost as far as the progress they make each year. While awaiting arrival of the ideal, perhaps the best approach is the second-best: developing and widely promulgating practice guidelines, protocols of treatment based on clinical trials and other empirical evidence. We'll look further into the problem of increasing the certainty of medical knowledge in Chapter 8.

All of those considerations complicate the effort to maximize quality while achieving the lowest possible cost. It has been said that where money is con-

TABLE 4.2   Health Expenditures, Selected Nations, 1996

	Per Capita	% of GDP
U.S.	$3,898	14.0
Canada	$2,065	9.6
Great Britain	$1,317	6.9
Germany	$2,278	10.5
Japan (1995)	$1,677	7.2

Source: OECD Health 98, Paris, OECD, 1998.

cerned, what counts is what can be counted, and the costs of care are a lot easier to quantify than the benefits. Which leads us to the second leg of the
trilemma tripod: cost control.

Health Care Costs: How High the Moon?

What Americans want is low-cost care. What they have is the highest costs in
the world. A quick comparison (see Table 4.2), using 1996 figures (public statistics always become publicly available a year or more after the period covered), reveals the size of the cost gap.

If we then refer back to the infant mortality and life expectancy figures given
earlier, we have to ask: Why are U.S. costs so much higher? Are there justifica-
tions in other measures of quality or in broader access to care? As we'll see further on, these are not easy questions to answer.

International comparisons are of interest to policy wonks, comparative political scientists, and public health officials. But they did not cause the national
angst about cost that has developed over the rapid pace of U.S. health cost increases in the past three to four decades. The demand for cost control has
arisen from rates of health care cost increases far outpacing general inflation
(see Table 4.3) and from the increasing share of institutional resources gobbled
up to feed the seemingly insatiable health care delivery system appetite. Both
major sets of payers, private employers and government agencies, are the vitally concerned parties, financially speaking, whereas individual Americans are
the medically concerned parties.

Corporations have seen health care change from a minor employee benefit
cost hardly worth top management's notice into an 800-pound gorilla. In 1996,
the big three auto firms (Ford, General Motors, and Chrysler) spent $6.7 billion
on employee health care. That's more than they spent on steel. Health benefit
cost inflation explains why employers became adamant that the cost picture

TABLE 4.3   National Health Expenditures, 1960–1996, Aggregate (in Billions) and Per Capita

	1960	1970	1980	1990	1995	1996
Aggregate	$26.9	$73.2	$247.3	$699.5	$991.4	$1,035.1
Per Capita	141	341	1,052	2,691	3,633	3,759

Source: Office of the Actuary, Health Care Financing Administration, as presented in Katharine R. Levit et al., in *Health Affairs* 17, No. 1 (Jan/Feb 1998), pp. 35–51.

had to change and why they have been pulling and pushing their employees into HMOs and other managed care plans where costs are lower. It has to be noted, however, that many analysts see the lesser cost increase rates of HMOs to be a temporary, one-time result of moving employees out of FFS and reducing their rates of hospitalization, which is the most frequently noted difference in utilization of resources between the two types. Premiums paid by employers increased 352 percent between 1970 and 1980. In the next decade, they rose 6–8 percent annually, and by 1990 they were back into double digit growth.

By 1997 a major survey found an average health benefit cost of $3,924 per employee, and by the end of that year traditional indemnity insurance covered only 15 percent of workers. The typical worker's share of premium costs was zero 20 years ago, but was $1,596 a year for subsidized family coverage in 1996.[10]

The national government was burdened until the mid-1990s by rising national deficits brought on by slower national income gains since the early 1970s, the 1981 tax cut, and high defense spending. Since the Reagan administration, voter sentiment has also been rising against taxes and for a balanced budget, culminating in the Balanced Budget Act of 1997. The population is aging, and Social Security pension costs are rising. Medicare and Medicaid cost, however, are rising faster, so it is the latter programs that Washington identifies as the culprits. I examine their problems in Chapter 5.

The most personal of health care expenses is, ironically, the one least discussed in health policy literature: what each American pays out-of-pocket (OOP). Some 1995 projections indicated that persons below age 65 spent 8 percent of income OOP, whereas seniors averaged 21 percent.[11] A recent projection shows the same 21 percent in 1997 for FFS beneficiaries, but 16 percent for those in HMOs. This translates into an overall average of $2,149 annually for all Medicare enrollees but $2,454 for those in FFS and $1,775 for those in HMOs.[12]

An average (a mean) is not a median, however, and there is an interesting financial-political footnote here. The top 1 percent of all persons with health care expenditures account for 30 percent of the spending, and the sickest 10 percent of Medicare patients account for 70 percent of that program's outlays, so OOP is equivalently concentrated.[13] For example, Medicare patients with family income over $30,000, living at home, averaged $883 in OOP in 1992, but those in long-term care facilities averaged $16,793.[14] Because the great majority of beneficiaries are not in long-term facilities, we can understand why there is not the political uproar one might expect if a substantial segment of seniors had out-of-pocket expenses as large as the overall average indicates—especially when one recalls that a quarter of Medicare beneficiaries have incomes below 150 percent of the poverty level. Still, if individuals were as organized as employers and government institutions, more attention would surely be paid to the insurance gaps, private and public, that produce the rather startling OOP figures. Once again, consumer-patients are the quiet stakeholders.

· Despite DRG and RVS caps, government expenditures have risen notably faster than private sector equivalents in recent years. In the period 1990–1996, the public costs rose from $284.4 billion to $483.1 billion, whereas private health expenditures went from $415.1 billion to $552 billion. This changes the public share of the total from 41 to 47 percent.[15] The Congressional Budget Office projects that by the year 2008 public and private sector health expenditures will each account for half of the total, an astounding development in a nation that prides itself on not having a government health care system![16]

Is the Insured Population Increasing? No

In a U.S. population of approximately 270 million people, over 16 percent—43.4 million people—were without either private or public health insurance coverage in 1997. Bad enough. But is the situation at least improving? No. In 1990 the uninsured figure was a bit under 36 million, and in 1980 it was about 29 million. After steady increases in the medically insured population from the 1930s through the immediate post–World War II decades, the United States has regressed disgracefully. Unless Americans do something major and soon, the worst may be yet to come: A 1996 American Hospital Association report projected that the uninsured figure will be 46 million people by 2002.[17]

Who are the uninsured? The aged? No. Only 1 percent of the over-65 age group is not in Medicare. The unemployed? They constitute less than half of those lacking coverage. Families headed by full-year, full-time workers compose 57 percent of the uninsured, and another 8 percent are in families with part-time workers.[18] The uninsured are basically low-income, low-education *working* men and women, mostly in businesses with fewer than 25 employees or working part-time, plus their children. Smaller employers and marginal firms are least likely to provide coverage. In 1980, 75 percent of firms paid the entire cost of their employees' health insurance; in 1995, about 35 percent did. Employers have been steadily increasing the share of premium costs charged to their employees. In 1992–1996 employee contributions went up twice as much as did employers' premium costs.[19] By 1996, workers in large firms paid 30 percent of family coverage costs; those in smaller firms paid 44 percent.[20] Even with employees paying more, employment-based coverage had declined to 61 percent by 1996 from 67 percent in 1990 and is almost certainly still declining. And now early retirees (those retiring before age 65 and thus not eligible for Medicare) are rapidly losing employer coverage.[21]

How about children? Private coverage has declined from 73 percent in 1989 to 66 percent in 1995, most of the drop a function of reduced employer coverage for dependents, and the 15 percent of children under 18 without insurance—nearly 11 million kids—is the highest proportion since 1987.[22] The situation would be much worse if Medicaid had not started picking up some of the slack, thanks in large part to a persevering and politically agile House health subcommittee chairman, Henry Waxman. He pushed legislation that brings children under Medicaid even when the family is not otherwise eligible, covering children through age 13 in below-poverty income families as of 1996 and slated to cover through age 18 by 2002. Added good fortune is the $24 billion State Child Health Insurance Program that may add up to 3.4 million kids to the covered category over the next five years through a variety of state-designed programs.[23] Also, a special effort got under way in 1998 to bring into Medicaid more of the 4.7 million children eligible but not enrolled. Perhaps 2 million or more of these children were made eligible under the Waxman-stimulated expansions, but the good word is apparently not being well distributed.[24]

Some respond to the uninsured data by saying, "Well, don't they get care anyway—just by going to the nearest emergency room?" Not exactly. Federal law requires that a hospital not turn away anyone in unstable, life-threatening condition, but that requirement doesn't cover most health needs. A summary of several studies done in the 1990s concludes that those without insurance "have less access to care, use less care, cannot obtain specific health care services, are twice as likely to be hospitalized for conditions that can be averted by outpatient care . . . and have a higher risk of death when they go into the hospital."[25]

A 1996 Urban Institute study sponsored by the American College of Physicians concluded that lack of insurance was associated with a 25 percent higher risk of death, and that uninsured injured children were 27 percent less likely to receive treatment than insured children.[26] Analysis of the care of 49,000 children in 1993–1994 found that having health insurance correlated strongly with access to primary care: 22 percent of uninsured children went without needed medical or dental care, versus 6 percent of the insured; 84 percent of the insured had contact with a physician in the preceding year, versus 67 percent of the uninsured.[27]

If outcomes are the primary medical test for quality in the medical services and procedures done by physicians, the percentage of the population insured is surely a proper test for quality of a health care "delivery system." By that measure, the United States definitely does not set the quality pace, for it is the only industrial nation apart from South Africa that does not have a health care framework providing coverage for all or nearly all of its population.

Although I contend that universal coverage is a sine qua non, two significant limitations have to be noted. The first is the one for which we each bear some degree of personal responsibility: No health care system can be expected to obviate the need for taking care of our bodies. Tobacco, fatty diets, lack of exercise, and alcohol are major killers in the United States. If we all began to do what we could individually to improve our health, there would be less need for medical interventions to repair the damage, and lower costs, too.

Secondly, it is clear that social stratification plays a major role in the use and effectiveness of the health care system, and not just in the United States. In the United Kingdom, despite a half century of the National Health Service, statistics show a definite positive correlation between what sociologists call SES (socioeconomic status—income, education, and occupation) and health status.[28] All sorts of cultural factors also play roles in how and how much we use the health care delivery system—from long-established folk medicine regimes (some of which are now being recognized by mainstream medicine) through religious prohibitions. The bottom line remains that unless one has coverage, one lacks the opportunity to make the best use of the system.

So, What's the Trilemma?

Having sketched the various meanings of quality, the parameters of expenses, and the problems of coverage, we are now ready to address the trilemma. The question to ask yourself is, How much of the desired value of any one factor am I willing to forego to have more of the others? It will not be an easy choice to make.

Let's first pair maximum access and lowest cost, the combination farthest from what Americans actually have. This pairing would mean adding coverage for 42 million more people while cutting the per capita cost to, say, the level of Canada and Germany, which would mean reducing expenditures by about 40 percent. One does not have to be the proverbial "rocket scientist" (why is that occupation always used as shorthand for high intelligence? Aren't there equally bright people in many other fields—even, dare one say it, in political science?) to forecast the ineluctable result. Because we know that the uninsured currently receive less care, we must assume some increase in demand. But we are also looking for ways to make deep reductions in expenditures. So what would have to happen is a deep cut in quality.

Can't the system just be more efficient? Of course, but managed care companies have been trying that route for a number of years now with only marginal success. Consolidations and mass purchasing of supplies will never produce the savings this scenario would require. We would have to think the unthinkable to accomplish the combination suggested. One unthinkable would be to establish a greatest-good-for-the-greatest-number priority. In this scenario, if, say, $30,000 can either do one complicated surgical procedure or can extend care for ordinary health problems to several hundred previously uninsured patients, the latter need would prevail and the surgery would not be performed. Even if such a trade-off would be publicly acceptable, the United States has no institutional mechanism for making it.

Another pair of unthinkables might be marginally more palatable because they would be less publicly visible and would not pit identifiable individuals against one another. It is widely accepted among health system observers that technological changes may well be the largest driver of increasing health care costs, so one idea is a sharp reduction in federally funded basic medical research. The other is a strict technology assessment program that proscribes new technologies, whether a surgical procedure or a mode of treatment, unless they meet some sort of cost-benefit test. Radical steps? Yes, but even such measures would not accomplish the maximum access/lowest cost combination without sacrifice of much that Americans now identify as indicators of medical quality.

A number of less drastic but surely helpful steps could also be taken to ease the crunch—things Americans should be doing more of now if they really gave a priority to health care for all. They could make far more extensive use of physician assistants, nurse practitioners, and midwives—professionals with less training than physicians but fully capable of successfully handling a substantial fraction of everyday complaints that patients present for treatment. In fact, some HMOs already accredit some nurses as primary care providers, although not without complaint from physicians. Americans could make far broader use of county public health clinics and community health centers like the federally subsidized ones that have operated since the 1960s. One of the promising recent developments in delivering low-cost, effective care is the mobile unit that draws up on a scheduled day to a school, a housing project, or a church. The Greater Hollywood Health Partnership, a consortium of 18 churches, has succeeded in preventing a lot of expensive ER visits through its foundation-supported program. It finds that people are less hesitant about accepting flu shots or screenings at their familiar churches than about going to hospitals or physicians' offices. A great program, but hard to expand very far. Only a real paradigm shift in the U.S. medical culture would enable the country to move to a lower-cost system while achieving universal health insurance without much sacrifice in expected aspects of what Americans call quality.

How about maximum access/maximum quality? If we assume a substantial increase in costs to cover the presently uninsured and continue the rest of the system at its present levels of service and costs, then overall costs will rise, not fall. That's the last thing that either employers or governments will countenance. It would mean squeezing out other domestic programs as health's share of state and federal budgets increased. Medicare and Medicaid costs rise faster than inflation even without additional patients being covered in the public sector system. The predictable cost increases of this scenario rule it out completely.

We are left with maximum quality/lowest cost. This combination involves moving even further away from universal coverage. Why would the uninsured number increase? On the public side, states can save money by raising the income bar for Medicaid eligibility, throwing more adults off the rolls. Private employers, striving always to reduce employee health benefit costs, are already approaching a bottom limit of the discounts they can squeeze out of insurers and HMOs (and they, in turn, out of hospitals and doctors). The alternate route, already clearly being taken, is to reduce coverage. This reduction is accomplished by eliminating dependents and by increasing deductibles, copayments, and the employees' share of premiums, probably leading to de facto underinsurance as employees react by not obtaining treatment for less-serious problems.

Maximum quality/lowest cost is, in fact, the implicit choice Americans now make. While quietly allowing the uninsured to do without much helpful, even necessary, care, Americans emphasize doing everything possible for those with insurance coverage. "Everything possible" is not the same as doing all that is reasonable, if one defines reasonable by such indicators as having a good chance of returning a patient to normal functioning or keeping a person alive for a substantial period of time rather than just delaying death a few hours or days.

Neonatology provides a good example of how quality as technological wizardry drives up health care costs. Until very recently, low birthweight babies could not be saved. Newborn specialists understandably push the envelope, so Americans now save many more, with medical success defined as how low a birthweight can survive. What neonatology does not do is take into account the lifetime costs, in constant medical expenditure and in family strain, of saving a life, in many cases, without any expectation of achieving normal functioning.

At the other end of the life cycle, does it make sense to extend care for pneumonia to a terminal cancer patient with a life expectancy measured in days or weeks? It often "makes sense" to the patient's family because Medicare (i.e., the taxpayers) and usually a Medigap insurance policy pay the bill, and the family thinks only of the presumed benefit. For those under 65 and lacking insurance, such decisions are made less generously.

American medical culture is aggressive: Americans ask for antibiotics for head colds, knowing that they will be ineffective. One physician has written that for most doctors, "the dictum *primum non nocere* ('first, do no harm') is replaced by 'first, do something.'"[29] Even when patients file advance directives (living wills, durable power of attorney for health affairs) stating that they do not want extraordinary measures taken to keep them alive, those instructions are ignored perhaps one-third of the time. What people and providers in more financially disciplined (and often more fiscally strapped) systems would call "prolonging death" Americans call "extending life," apparently paying less attention to the quality of the life being extended.

Does all that sound harsh? It does to me, because I am used to defining medical quality in part as avoiding death at any expense. Other nations do not—and recognize that they cannot afford to—practice by such an ethic. Equal access to medical care is sacrificed in the United States to a combination of both higher expectations than anywhere else and a largely open-ended set of employer- and government-funded entitlements to care.

Open-ended? Hasn't managed care put a stop to that? It has reduced the diameter of the health care spigot, but it has not fundamentally changed the U.S. medical culture. Trying to reduce the system's costs while fulfilling Americans' medical expectations is precisely the cause of the current anguish. Trying simultaneously to maximize access would simply underline the absolute impossibility of achieving the tripartite goal.

Here's a summary of how the various components stand today: For the elderly, Medicare's fee-for-service program, in which one can find out who's the best surgeon at the best hospital and get on her or his list for the triple bypass, can offer high quality, but its costs are ballooning rapidly despite several cost control strategies adopted since the late 1980s. At working ages, employment-based health care has in recent years stanched the flow of dollars through use of managed care, but quality is perhaps threatened for the sickest of HMO members. In addition, the proportion of the population covered has been declining. Through most of the earlier health care history of the United States, quality for those with deep pockets or expensive health insurance has been the top goal, implicitly, and both access and cost suffered. In no form of delivery has the United States been able to achieve anything close to universal coverage, despite having the highest costs in the world. And the market can *never* achieve universal coverage on its own, for costs will never be zero.

We face a trilemma—a triple set of interrelated dilemmas. How does it relate to the basic dilemma set forth in Chapter 1? I said there that Americans' twin goals are to provide the best care to everyone while keeping government out of the picture. If Americans explicitly abandoned the access-for-everyone goal, the dilemma would disappear: They would sell health care as a market good (i.e., ration it by price), and some would have it while many would not—just like cars, houses, and all other consumer goods. Americans could cut off the other horn instead: use government to establish a national framework for universal health coverage by mandating employer and employee contributions to a privately operated system, as in Germany (see Chapter 6), or switch most health care costs to the public sector directly by expanding Medicare to the entire population, just like old age pensions under Social Security. So long as Americans stick to the irreconcilable aims of wanting the best care for everyone and forbidding government to fill in where the private sale and purchase of health care cannot do the job, they will be faced with the trilemma on which this chapter has focused.

What pluses and minuses would you list for each combination? Should one goal be largely forgotten to maximize the other two? Which one? Why? Or should we try to define a middle ground among the three goals? What indicators can be used to define the compromise positions? Who will do the defining? What role can or should government play in rationalizing the system, keeping in mind that a bit over half of the health care expenditures in the United States are made in the private sector, without any widely accepted focal policy point?

5

Medicare and Medicaid

The Entitlement Dilemmas

Baden Medical Services rural clinic. Alicia Estevez and two-year-old daughter check out. Poor family, no medical assistance. Photo courtesy of the Image Works, © Steven Rubin, reprinted with permission.

M<small>EDICARE HAS AS MANY LIVES AS A CAT.</small> Every time the latest projection shows it running out of money, Congress does something to save it for a few years more. A recent dire prediction was of insolvency in 2001, but the latest fixes, contained in the Balanced Budget Act of 1997, push that date forward to 2007. Incumbent national legislators may now breathe easier as they contemplate their next election campaigns, but Americans need to be aware of the problems that are simply being postponed and of additional ones that the nation has hardly begun to recognize, let alone deal with.

The most basic fact about Medicare and Medicaid is that they are government-financed and organized programs and thus exceptions to the private market health care delivery system. So seamlessly has Medicare (much more so than Medicaid) been woven into the fabric of American health care that some seniors who use it, and adult children who rely on it for their aging parents, can rail against government health care without realizing the contradiction in what they are saying. Rare are the voices of any who would repeal these programs, and the fundamental reason is clear: political recognition three decades ago that most of the elderly, plus the nonelderly poor, could not afford doctor and hospital fees. During the rapid growth of employer-subsidized care in the post–World War II years and with Medicare and Medicaid seemingly providing an adequate answer for the elderly and the poor, market-based financing was not as problematic as it has become in recent years. Employers and governments are both balking at the price tag (which keeps ratcheting up), and medicine keeps improving and becoming even more indispensable. Therefore, the "rely on the market" mantra that now dominates dicta on health care becomes every more clearly inadequate, at either the employer-provided or the individual private purchaser level. In terms of the basic dilemma presented in Chapter 1, Medicare and Medicaid are therefore the largest explicit recognition that the United States has to ignore (or transcend, as you wish) the "keep government out of it" ideology half of the choice if Americans are to even come close to meeting the positive goal of universal coverage.

Medicare and Medicaid passed Congress together in 1965, but their paths were politically quite different. Medicare, a universal program for persons age

65 or more, regardless of income, is the residue of abortive efforts over many years to pass universal health insurance. Seniors were an attractive target population: people generally beyond their working years, who had a 1967 poverty rate of 30 percent, compared with 13 percent for the rest of the population.[1] In the late 1990s, their poverty rate is about the same as for the rest of the population, perhaps even slightly lower, but Medicare is solidly entrenched as a social insurance program. Everyone pays into it, and everyone receives its benefits.

Medicaid, conversely, represents not the culmination of years of advocacy but an ironic political accident. It operates as a joint federal-state program, with a majority of the money coming from Washington but with the responsibility for running it part of the state governments. Medicare and Medicaid are sufficiently different so that I will take up each separately.

What Does Medicare Cost the Taxpayers? The Seniors?

Reflecting a variety of political struggles among competing health care interests, one segment of Medicare (Part A) covers the use of hospitals, whether as in- or out-patient. Part B covers physicians' services, laboratory tests, and certain preventive screening exams—Pap smears, mammograms, and (added in 1997) prostate and colon cancer tests. Home health services are being transferred from Part A to Part B over six years, a change initiated in 1997, both because such services really fit better there and as a way to relieve the Part A trust fund of a fast-growing financial obligation. There are two very important health expenses that Medicare does *not* cover: prescription medications and long-term nursing home care. (Table 5.1 provides more coverage detail.)

Because Part A is funded by a payroll tax in the working years, Medicare is called a contributory social insurance program rather than part of welfare, but that characterization is only partly true. Part B is 25 percent funded by enrollee premiums but 75 percent funded out of general revenues. So three-fourths of Part B is in the same financing category as means-tested Medicaid—a fact that some defenders of Medicare who also oppose noncontributory tax transfers to the poor like to ignore.

Medicare payments for services are based on "allowed charges," which once meant "usual, customary, and reasonable." Since the mid-1980s the allowed charges generally mean a fixed fee set by the DRG scale or the RVS, usually considerably lower than the provider's listed charge for the service. There are also substantial deductibles and time limits on hospital and skilled nursing home stays. Within such limits, Medicare pays all of hospitalization for 60 days

TABLE 5.1   Medicare Coverage (Fee-for-Service)

Hospital Insurance (Part A)

In-patient stays up to 16 days, plus a "lifetime reserve" of 60 days
Skilled nursing facility care, up to 100 days, after having been hospitalized at least 3 days
(Note: Number of days given is per "benefit period," which begins the day you enter a facility and ends when you have been out of the facility for 60 straight days.)
Home health care (Transfer to Part B over 6 years)
Hospice care
Out-patient hospital services

Medical Services (Part B)

Medically necessary services of a doctor
Laboratory tests
Ambulance transportation
Home health care (1998 begins transfer from Part A)
Screening tests (pap smear, mammograms, etc.)
Durable medical equipment

Services Not Covered

Prescription drugs, except for in-patients
Hearing aids
Dentures
Routine physicals

Source: Health Care Financing Administration, www.hcfa.gov.

and 80 percent of allowed charges for Part B (mostly physician) services. What Medicare does not pay is the responsibility of the patient, and two-thirds of Medicare subscribers purchase "Medigap" (i.e., supplementary) private insurance to cover the remainder of allowed charges. See Table 5.2.

Now let's use some numbers to get a sense of Medicare's demographic dimensions and its financial trend line. In 1975, Medicare had 21.8 million aged (over-65) enrollees; in 1997, 33 million. It also had 5 million permanently and totally disabled persons of any age and 300,000 persons needing kidney dialysis for end stage renal disease (ESRD) in 1997. Medicare's total enrollment was thus over 38 million people.

The basic fact behind Medicare's expanding enrollment is that the aged population is rising at a significantly faster pace than the under-65 group. In the 1990–1996 period, the under-65s increased by 6 percent and the over-65 group increased by 8 percent. Taking a longer perspective, since 1900 (thanks much more to improved public health than to individual medical treatment and technology) the proportion of over-65 Americans has grown from 4.1 per-

TABLE 5.2   Medicare Costs to Patient, 1998

Part A

Hospital in-patient deductible $764
  $190 a day for days 61 through 90
  $382 a day for each lifetime reserve day
Skilled nursing facility
  20 days without charge
  $95.50 a day for days 21 through 100
Out-patient hospital services: 20 percent of what hospital charges

Part B

Deductible $100 per year
Patient pays 20% copayment medical services
Monthly premium $43.80
Home health services and tests—no charge

Source: Health Care Financing Administration, www.hcfa.gov.

cent to 12.8 percent. They are living longer (a person who turned 65 in 1996 had a life expectancy of 17.7 more years), so the elderly are themselves getting older. The 65–74 group has increased 8 times since 1900, but the over-85 group has increased 31 times and now numbers nearly 4 million. Projections indicate that by 2030, the elderly will be one-fifth of the population.[2] Steady expansion of Medicare's clientele is assured! Furthermore, as the population ages, the over-65 contingent accounts for an ever-increasing share of health expenditures. For example, the over-65 group constituted 11 percent of the population in 1980 and 29 percent of health spending. By the year 2040, one projection is that 45 percent of national health expenditures will be used for the 21 percent of the population that will then be 65 and above.[3]

Medicare's expenditures for services began at $3.4 billion in fiscal 1967 and quickly ballooned, reaching $37.5 billion in 1980, $112.1 billion in 1990, and $203.1 billion in 1996. The swiftness of the rise resulted in good part from a political trade-off. Fearing that the AMA's opposition to the legislation would translate into a physician boycott—an embarrassment that President Johnson would not risk—Congress deliberately avoided building in any cost controls. To pay what was "usual, customary, and reasonable" turned out to be an invitation to providers to raise rates year by year, each raise then being added in to the "usual and customary" base, which in turn de facto defined what was taken to be reasonable. It took nearly 20 years before budgetary pressures were strong enough to provide political cover for prospective payment systems to be put in place. As the prospective payment systems took hold in the mid-1980s,

TABLE 5.3   Rates of Use Per 10,000 Elderly Persons, Selected Procedures

	1976	*1980*	*1986*	*1993*
Catheterization	15.2	32.6	94.7	148.0
Bypass surgery	5.3	15.0	42.9	79.2
Angioplasty	0.0	0.0	7.1	52.1

Source: National Center for Health Statistics, Centers for Disease Control.

Medicare's average annual rate of growth declined from 17.3 percent, 1975–1985, to 9.8 percent, 1985–1997. Even the lower figures continue to show a growth rate far exceeding that of the Consumer Price Index (CPI). Medicare's lateness in adopting meaningful cost controls is a major reason why it has so greatly exceeded the overall CPI.

Another important reason for the higher growth rate of medical services lies in the secular trend of what is called greater "intensity of care," which is well illustrated with an anecdote from the pre–World War II years showing a contrast in

the histories of two patients with similar types of heart disease. One was recorded in 1908; the other at the same hospital in 1938. The total written record of the first patient occupied 2.5 pages, and the observations represented the combined efforts of two physicians, the attending and the house officer, and of one specialist, the pathologist-bacteriologist. The record of the second patient . . . comprised 29 pages and represented the combined observations of three visiting physicians, two residents, three house officers, ten specialists, and fourteen technicians.[4]

And intensity has greatly increased in the postwar years, as biomedical knowledge and technology have advanced by leaps and bounds.

A significant portion of greater intensity results from the rapid diffusion of newly developed technologies and procedures—often before their value has been proven. Although the unit cost of each operation often goes down as a procedure moves from the experimental stage to routine use, the volume goes up, rapidly and considerably. For examples, see Table 5.3.

The explosion in the use of and expenditures for home health care and skilled nursing facilities (SNFs) has been of particular concern in the 1990s. Contrast Medicare's overall 9.8 percent expenditure growth rate annually between 1985 and 1995 with that of SNFs at 32.5 percent and home health care at 22.8 percent.

The average annual expenditure per Medicare beneficiary was $6,716 in 1992, compared to $2,159 that year for the non-Medicare population. However, usage is highly concentrated among a minority of enrollees. Because services become more intense as death approaches, it is not surprising that the 6 percent who die in a given year account for one-fifth of all payments. ESRD patients are only 0.68 percent of enrollees but account for 5.6 percent of Medicare payments. In the overall population, the top 1 percent of persons having health care expenditures accounted for 30 percent of aggregate costs in 1987. Nearly half of that group were elderly, so these patterns have a considerable overlap.

As the 65-plus population increases—particularly as the baby boom generation reaches Medicare age—it is inescapable that the volume of Medicare services will expand. The Congressional Budget Office estimates that Medicare spending will grow to $277 billion in 2002 and to $448 billion by 2008, the rate of increase averaging 8.3 percent annually between 2002 and 2008.[5] As a percent of the federal budget—a politically crucial fact—Medicare will grow from under 12 percent in 1997 to 16 percent in 2008. Medicare was only 3.7 percent in 1970.

For years, budget cuts concentrated on those programs dependent on annual appropriations (discretionary spending), whereas entitlements (open-ended expenditures to pay for all legislated benefits) were largely immune. But with discretionary programs already substantially reduced, it is clear that the big savings will have to come from entitlements. Furthermore, with passage of the Balanced Budget Act of 1997, intense pressure exists to keep the federal budget figure on target so that Republicans and Democrats can show that they have actually balanced the budget. Also, it is likely that further changes intended to slow expenditure growth will be made as Congress gets closer to facing the cost implications of the boomers reaching Medicare age. How to control costs thus becomes a more important question every year.

The Balanced Budget Act mandates considerable expansion of prospective payment techniques as a way to limit Medicare payments to providers. Skilled nursing facilities began transition to prospective payment in 1998; hospital outpatient services (whose continuation of open-ended charges has been one of the largest gaps in cost control) were to begin PPS on January 1, 1999; and home health agencies and inpatient rehabilitation facilities were to begin in October 1999. Nor do physicians escape unscathed: the Volume Performance Standard in the fee schedule system is being changed in 1999 to a "sustainable growth rate" system, pegging spending growth to growth of the general economy.

These changes reflect the legislators' fear of the wrath of seniors, whose voting rate is higher than other age groups and who tend to make protection of Medicare benefits a single-issue test for candidates. Congress and presidents have found it expedient to cut hospital and physician reimbursements while leaving benefit eligibility and cost-sharing largely alone. However, it is apparently now thought that it will be necessary to spread the cost-cutting pain to beneficiaries to a greater degree than in the past.

This became clear in 1997 when the Senate grasped the third rail of American politics and survived: The upper house voted to change Medicare eligibility from age 65 to 67 (as is already in the works for Social Security under changes legislated in 1983) and charge significantly higher Part B premiums to higher income enrollees. The vote was not matched in the House and did not survive budget negotiations, but it has probably altered the health care landscape so that beneficiaries will soon have to share cost-increase pains with providers much more than in the past.

Proposing to make some seniors pay more or to make all seniors wait two more years before achieving eligibility would, of course, worsen the gap between the total expense for an individual's care and Medicare's share. Out-of-pocket (OOP) costs already take a big bite out of a 65-plus family's income. On average OOP was $2,519 per beneficiary in 1995, a substantial increase from 10 years earlier. Note, however, that the average hides a great variation. See Chapter 4.

Medicare: The Policy Dilemmas

The coming flood of boomers makes restraining Medicare costs a reasonable concern. The over-65 population was 33.9 million in 1996; it will be 53.2 million in 2020 and 69.4 million in 2030.[6] Tweaking the eligibility age or squeezing some extra dollars out of higher income enrollees are not the only issues, despite the media headlines and patient anguish they generate.

Other issues of great importance exist, not all of which have received much public attention. And they all confront Americans with difficult choices.

Is Medicare Really Ready for Managed Care?

The first difficult choice is this: Should seniors be encouraged, urged, pushed, or mandated into HMOs and other managed care arrangements and away from the traditional FFS system that still enrolls 85 percent of them?

Encouragement has been the government's choice for several years, but strangely so in light of evidence that the government is probably spending more on its HMO enrollees than on its FFS beneficiaries. HMO payments from Washington have been set at 95 percent of the average of Medicare payments in a given area, but many health plans have cleverly (from their bottom-line viewpoint) recruited members from among the most healthy seniors and can provide their care for 85 to 90 percent of the area average. When an HMO holds an information-and-sign-up opportunity at the site of a senior PGA golf tournament, those walking around following the action are not likely to be among the more ill of the over-65 individuals. By such devices, the cream is skimmed off the top of the patient mix.

Those remaining in fee-for-service Medicare then comprise a sicker-than-average population. They run up higher bills for Uncle Sam to pay, becoming an ever-stronger target for cost-cutting, which tends, so far, to mean reducing payments to physicians. At a point perhaps not too far off, those physicians not dependent on a cadre of Medicare patients for their income (not a large proportion) may decide to post signs politely declining to serve them, as happened to Medicaid enrollees for a number of years.

So why are the Feds pushing managed care enrollments? They are betting on the future, apparently. At the same time that 1997 legislation tries to entice seniors to move to managed care by approving looser kinds of arrangements—PPOs, POSs, Provider Service Organizations (PSOs), and Medical Savings Accounts (MSAs)—steps are also being taken to rectify the payment anomaly. Small demonstrations are planned to test competitive bidding for Medicare senior HMO contracts, which is the way to go if the Feds are to catch up to the private sector.

The policy dilemma is that the attempt to shift Medicare patients into managed care coincides with considerable public anguish about the side effects of moving medicine from the individualism of old to the large-scale organizations developing today. The patients that legislators are courting with bills to "protect" them are predominantly under-65 people enrolled in plans through their employers. It seems likely that people over 65 would need even more help to navigate their way through managed care, many of them knowing only decades of traditional medicine: one patient, one doctor to relate to, by free choice.

Indeed, both members of Congress and Medicare administrators indicated great concern over the problem of explaining to the elderly the different plans available under Medicare + Choice as the fall 1998 date approached for sending comparative information to each senior. The details of such comparisons are said to be daunting even for sophisticated beneficiaries, yet the Medicare population includes perhaps 20 percent with Alzheimer's or other mental impairments, plus many with poor eyesight or limited literacy skills. Further problems will predictably arise after 2003, when seniors who switch from FFS to one of the newer options will no longer be allowed to switch back on one month's notice. Instead, they will only be able to switch during the first three months of each year.

In these circumstances, is it sensible to make managed care enrollment the centerpiece of Medicare's cost containment efforts at this time? Or has the cart been hitched ahead of the horse? That may be the case, to judge by some studies, such as one in 1997 of Medicare patients switching back and forth between HMOs and FFS, whose authors titled their journal article, "The Medicare-HMO Revolving Door—The Healthy Go in and the Sick Go Out."[7] Perhaps HCFA should first push *itself* vigorously to establish a competitive bidding system for HMOs so that it can really save money, or at least ratchet down its payments in areas where basing them on traditionally high FFS fees has produced windfalls for health plan entrepreneurs and freebies for some seniors.

Tightened reimbursements mandated by Congress in 1997 began to cause reductions in prescription drug coverage (the most desired of HMO extras) by mid-1998. By the end of the year a major problem emerged as senior HMOs began to pull out of counties in which they estimated they could not make a profit. In a number of cases, especially in rural areas, this meant a scramble by seniors to find another HMO or return to FFS Medicare. And that creates great difficulty for many who may not be able to afford a Medigap policy to cover the larger copayments facing them as they move out of HMOs.

Does all that controversy make it sound as though HCFA should just abandon managed care? Not at all, for American medicine is clearly not going to return to the FFS pattern. There *are* substantial efficiencies of scale to be had from large physician groups and the best managed care organizations, and they can provide certain medical advantages, such as continuity of care, integrated specialist services, preventive care, and health education. (See Chapter 7 for the pros and cons of managed care.) But the costs advantage of HMOs will only work for Medicare if HCFA switches to competitive bidding by such health plans.

So there's the first dilemma: Can the government, despite all the foot-dragging associated with long-standing bureaucracies, move nimbly enough to create a managed care system that will save money and achieve the potential health benefits of group care yet avoid problems arising from the revolution in health care organization?

Close the Open-Ended Entitlement?

We move on to a more explosive issue. The government has issued a blank check for the Medicare entitlement, not bound by specific annual appropriations, to cover all needed care within the Medicare policy framework. Some politicians and think tank economists would put a stop to the open-ended commitment, replacing it with a fixed dollar sum per enrollee per year. Such a change could take the form of "cafeteria" plans in which one has a choice among plans on an approved list (which is the model of health benefits for federal employees), but the best plans may require a premium beyond the sum paid by Medicare. Or, in a more privatized version, there could be vouchers with which beneficiaries would enter the private health care market to fare as best they could.

Corporate health benefits have been moving in the same direction: An array of plans is offered, and the employer puts up a fixed sum to be applied against whichever plan the employee chooses. Choice of a plain vanilla plan will not require any extra payment; choice of a Mercedes-level plan will.

The great plus of fixed federal health contributions (from the federal government's viewpoint) would be that the federal government could control the extent to which its commitment increased each year. Instead of wondering if market developments would cause a 2 or 9 or 15 percent inflation in HCFA payments in a given fiscal year, the agency could set in advance a per beneficiary increase of its choosing. Proponents acknowledge that some safeguards would be in order for the elderly, a nontrivial number of whom have been conned by unscrupulous peddlers of Medigap policies. Presumably it would help to enact legislation similar to that used to make the Medigap competition more understandable and to require some minimum range of benefits in all plans offered.

Critics are dubious, especially of the voucher form, recognizing that the more vulnerable elderly may be duped by the least scrupulous of health plan salespersons. From being a patient to being an insurance negotiator is quite a leap to ask the over-65 person to make—especially 75- or 85-year-old people, most of whom did not have the younger generations' educational advantages. One can foresee cases of seniors signing up for policies that a salesman tells them cover some preexisting condition or contains some desired extras, but then finding no such coverage when the fine print is pointed out to them by a physician or hospital wanting payment for some service the policy did not cover. Who picks up the bill then? Do Americans, speaking through the government to which they assigned the task of providing a medical safety net for the elderly, say, "That's tough; you should have been a smarter consumer"? Or do they simply ask the hospital or doctor to write off the bill as bad debt and transfer that senior to Medicaid and out of Medicare, as punishment for not buying right? Not appealing prospects.

How Many Kinds of Medicare Do Americans Want?

Finally, should Medicare remain a single system, treating all enrollees alike, or is it acceptable to change it into a multioption, multitiered set of options?

Actually, Medicare beneficiaries belonging to HMOs do already have a different set of benefits from those in FFS, although the two-tier implications are rarely brought to the public's attention. The prescription, eye glass, health club, and other services not provided in traditional Medicare constitute a kind of "super Medicare." It is also possible that even those enjoying the freebies are paying a subtle price: Competitive pressures lead HMOs to offer the extras but also lead them to cut costs with draconian fervor. May not some seniors be short-changed on needed services so that the HMO can continue to afford freebies as a sales incentive? HMOs are an official alternative to FFS enrollment, but the freebies are not part of the services required to be a Medicare-approved HMO.

Some new programs in what the BBA of 1997 calls Medicare + Choice add tiers that include some far-reaching privatizing alternatives. One is to open up Medicare, on a trial basis, to Medical Savings Accounts (MSAs). In these plans, one puts tax-free contributions into a special savings account and purchases a high-deductible ($1,500-$6,000) major medical insurance policy. Medicare will pay for the insurance policy by contributing the average of its costs per beneficiary. If one stays healthy, does not use up one's savings account, and can afford to risk a high deductible policy, it may be a good deal.

Another new wrinkle permits a private contract between a doctor and a patient, a contract in which Medicare's fee schedule will not apply. The patient pays all bills, and no payment is made by Medicare for services included in such contracts. In effect, these contracts are a way to opt out of Medicare. A third form of privatization will be a private FFS kind of HMO: a curious hybrid of a plan that is like an HMO in receiving a per capita payment from Medicare for each enrollee, but in which the patient can then choose any provider and could be charged whatever they would accept, paying privately all beyond Medicare's monthly subsidy.

What appeals to well-off, healthy seniors and to some physicians and hospitals is that these options all avoid some or all of Medicare's regulation of fees and services, and some may save the enrollee money. If HCFA makes a contribution to an MSA or private plan at the average cost of care in an area, or close to that, then the private plan makes money and HCFA loses it, to the extent that the patient is healthy and does not use up the amount of the government contribution.

On the downside, these plans will attract enrollees, but probably at the eventual expense of taxpayers and FFS seniors. How so? First, the government will be making payments greater than the bills the healthier enrollees would have rung up in regular Medicare. With the healthiest beneficiaries siphoned off, the less healthy FFS enrollees will automatically have a higher per patient cost, creating pressure to cut costs in that program by putting even more pressure on providers and on enrollees in the form of higher Part B premiums.

A more basic concern is that these privatized alternatives can be seen as undermining the community-rated insurance principle on which Medicare is based. Over-individualized economics may assert that premiums should be attuned to individual risk, but that negates most of the function of insurance and, of greater societal importance, undermines the social solidarity principle of Medicare. As with Social Security pensions, this societal glue has given overwhelming political support to these programs. Which is more important: that Americans accommodate the wealthier, healthy seniors in their desire to privatize, or that they maintain as close to a single-tier Medicare system as they possibly can?

Medicaid: Medicare's Poor Relation

Medicaid, which has approximately 37 million enrollees, is commonly perceived as the program in each state that pays for health care for poor people, especially mothers and children who are on welfare. (Welfare eligibility is set at an income level far below poverty in most states, so more than half of the poor are left out.) The largest subniche automatically providing eligibility has been Aid to Families with Dependent Children (AFDC), popularly synonymous with "welfare," which was replaced in the 1996 welfare reform legislation by Temporary Assistance to Needy Families (TANF). TANF comprises 70 percent of Medicaid recipients, but these recipients represent only 30 percent of Medicaid expenditures. The second client group is the disabled, accounting for 15 percent of the people receiving Medicaid and 39 percent of expenditures. The third thrust of Medicaid covers the elderly poor in nursing homes, who now account for a third of Medicaid spending, though only a tenth of recipients. A substantial portion of the elderly poor are persons of formerly middle class income whose resources were exhausted by paying for nursing home care at the rate of more than $30,000 a year.

In recent years, the welfare-Medicaid linkage has been broken, so that children in families not fitting welfare income criteria are becoming eligible for

Medicaid. As of 1997, states must cover children under age 6 in families with incomes up to 133 percent of poverty, and children 6 to 13 with family incomes below the poverty level. (In many states, the eligibility level has been set considerably below the federally defined poverty level.) Mandatory coverage is scheduled to rise through age 18 by 2002. Ironically, as children's public sector coverage increases, so does the need for it, as more employers drop dependent coverage. Frustratingly, not all eligible children are enrolled, out of family ignorance, confusion about the changing relationship between Medicaid and welfare, and other factors. A May 1998 federal study produced the appalling estimate that as many as 4.7 million children may be eligible but not enrolled.[8]

Medicaid had total expenditures of $163 billion in 1996, of which Washington paid $92 billion (57 percent) and the states the remainder. The startling fact, contrary to popular perception, is that most of the money—about 61 percent—was spent on the aged and disabled group, while the poor children and parents received the remainder. Long-term care and the generally greater infirmities of late adulthood require much higher per-person payments for the elderly. In 1993, for example, $1,360 was spent on each child and $2,292 for an adult under 65, but $9,862 was spent per over-65 adult.[9] This anomaly is the result of Medicare's emphasis on acute care with little attention to the chronic care needs of the elderly. In 1965, the aging bulge in the population was not yet apparent, and medicine was not able to do as much to prolong life as it now can. But for the least healthy and very old people in the Medicare program, long-term care (LTC) in skilled nursing homes or room-and-board facilities is sometimes necessary for extended periods of time. Medicare's benefits are limited: After 20 days fully paid, there can be a maximum of 80 additional days, but each with a daily copayment of $95.50 (in 1998). Medicare patients therefore quickly become Medic*aid* patients by "spending down" their assets until they are in poverty. (We should note parenthetically that Medicare and Medicaid are "joined at the hip" for some of the elderly poor, for whom the law requires that states use their Medicaid programs to help pay the Medicare premiums and deductibles.)

The federal government and the states both saw their Medicaid budgets ballooning at double-digit inflation rates through the 1980s and part of the 1990s. Because of an improving economy in the mid-1990s and the adoption of managed care for Medicaid in many states, the rate of cost increase took a sharp drop in the late 1990s, but, as with Medicare, it remained above the CPI rate of increase. See Table 5.4.

The combination of ever-increasing costs and threats by the federal government to contain its majority share of Medicaid payments is creating an inter-

TABLE 5.4   Annual Percentage Growth Rate of Medicaid Expenditures, 1980–1996

	1980	1990	1993	1994	1995	1996
Federal	17.6	11.4	21.7	6.0	6.0	6.3
States	16.8	10.9	10.2	13.1	8.9	3.8

Source: National Health Accounts, Office of the Actuary, Health Care Financing Administration, as presented in Katharine R. Levit et al., in *Health Affairs* 17, No. 1 (Jan/Feb 1998), pp. 35–51.

generational problem in the states. Will equal attention be given to the LTC needs of the elderly and to children and adults in poverty? Or will political sympathy for the "fallen" middle class in board and care homes endanger an adequate level of care for the young poor and near poor? How should priorities be set in Medicaid? And by whom? The national government has so far met its share of the commitments it has itself created by law. But an aborted proposal in President Clinton's fiscal 1998 budget would have set a per person cap on the federal share, squeezing the states harder. In 1996 the Republican Congress and Democratic president combined to revamp the welfare system by, among other things, replacing an open-ended entitlement with a block grant that gives each state great discretion in designing its welfare-to-work program. Is that handwriting on the wall for Medicaid, too? Will or should Medicaid remain an entitlement program whose expenditures expand to meet medical demand? Or will both Medicaid and Medicare switch to annually fixed budgets?

As noted earlier in this chapter, long-term care is a need with a predictably strong rate of increase, given the fact of an aging population. The existing approach—private long-term care insurance policies for relatively affluent people and Medicaid for some of the poor and many middle class people who have exhausted their savings and moved into the poverty category as a result—is a makeshift way of handling the problem. As the boomers become part of the board-and-care patient base, the inadequacy of the bailing wire and glue approach will become all too manifest. Then politicians will pay strong attention to it in accord with the classic U.S. approach to policy making: respond to a crisis. The basic question is, Will the United States develop an LTC system that provides TLC for all its citizens by adding one more strand to the Social Security Act, or will Americans let long-term care become another area in which they leave to the market a need it cannot fill without governmental financing?

6

Good Health at
Lower Cost

How Do Other Nations Do It?

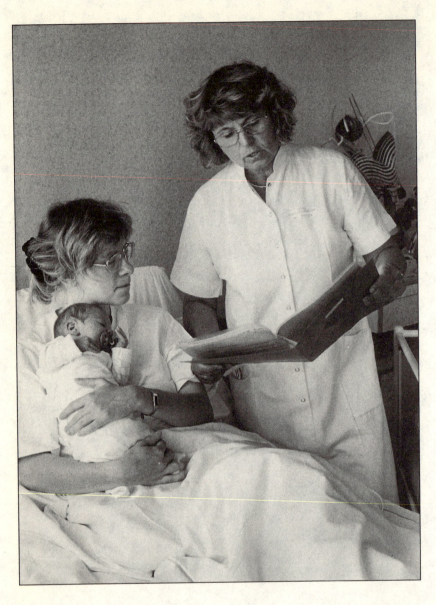

Nurse with mother and newborn baby in Germany. Photo courtesy of Monkmeyer Press Photo Service/Hugh Rogers, reprinted with permission.

BEFORE WE BEGIN TO EXPLORE THE variety of ways by which health care costs might be brought under control—and the issue of whether that really matters—it's time for a digression to see how other countries have designed their health care systems. If one knows only one's own way of doing something, one tends to think that is the only possible way. It rarely is. We'll sketch briefly the essential elements of the health systems of Canada, the United Kingdom, and Germany to learn something of the range of possibilities among industrial democracies. Within each, our three major points of interest will be

1. the mix of private and public elements,
2. the pattern of historical development, and
3. the approach to cost containment.

Canada: Mixed Funding and Provincial Responsibility

Canada, like the United States, has a federal form of government. The national government's role has been to establish a set of operational principles to which the regional governments (10 provinces, equivalent to states in the United States) must adhere in order to receive funding from Ottawa (seat of the federal government) for their health care programs. Within that framework, hospitals are nonprofit and receive annually negotiated lump sums from the provincial governments. Most physicians still operate independently, and half of them are general practitioners. The patient shows her or his insurance card (no copayment), then the doctor bills the provincial authority and receives a fee on a schedule negotiated between the regional medical association and the provincial Ministry of Health. The negotiation includes a firm cap on the totality of physician payments, so the doctors cannot make up in greater volume what they may lose in lower fees per service.

Because the money comes from a government, do patients lack choices or is a doctor's practice pattern micromanaged by "bureaucrats"? Not at all. Strange as it may seem (to an American, not a Canadian), both patients and doctors retain more traditional freedom than in the United States: HMOs, and even physician group practices, are only beginning to develop there. In the state-financed system, private insurance companies are not there to apply "utilization review" (UR) clearance systems to the providers, and patients make appointments directly with specialists of their choice. Lack of choice exists regarding when to undergo elective procedures, however, for Canada has waiting lists (queues, as they call them). Despite the governmentally set ceiling (at the level of the provinces) on total expenditures, the system is individualistically and privately operated at the level of medical practitioners. From a patient-doctor standpoint, it would not be much of a stretch to call it publicly financed private enterprise in health care.

Quiz question: What is the closest parallel in the United States? Answer: Fee-for-Service Medicare.

Six Decades of Federal Development

Justice Louis Brandeis wrote in a 1932 Supreme Court dissent that "it is one of the happy incidents of the federal system that a single courageous state may, if its citizens choose, serve as a laboratory; and try novel social and economic experiments without risk to the rest of the country."[1] Canada's health insurance programs are the result of exactly this kind of regional experimentation. The difference in the United States is that the experience with Kerr-Mills (see Chapter 2) at the state level proved the inadequacy of that program for the nation, whereas what the provinces started turned out to be a model for the Canadian nation.

Many pro-reform advocates in the United States are frustrated that even small steps toward universal coverage—such as expansions of children's coverage in recent years—take much politicking, development of public opinion, and time to achieve. They look North and see Canada's single-payer, universal, public health insurance system and would like to import it. But Canada did not get there quickly, either.

At Canada's beginning as a self-governing nation under the British North America Act of 1867, the hospitalization function was given to the provinces, on the premise that it was one of the less costly program areas. The premise proved to be false, but as responsibility for hospitals extended into all areas of health care, Canada gradually developed its interesting mix of provincial and national responsibilities for health care. Decision making for most of the operational dimensions of health care delivery is provincial, not national; however, those decisions must be made within a framework of principles embedded in national legislation. Funding is provided through both the national and provincial governments.[2] Canadian federalism thus stands in contrast to that of the United States, where the Constitution contains a supremacy clause for all areas in which the national government legislates.

The short story is that all of Canada achieved universal hospitalization insurance in 1960 and physician insurance in 1970. This system, one that meets with overwhelming approval in public opinion, traces its origins to 1909. The Saskatchewan provincial legislature then allowed municipalities to provide hospitals through local taxes. In 1914, it added general medical services. In British Columbia, strong sentiment for a national health insurance system developed in the legislature as early as 1919; by 1945, with polls showing 80 percent public approval for a national plan, all parties campaigned on health insurance platforms. No action was taken, however, until several provinces had established hospital plans that had a positive demonstration effect. National hospital insurance legislation was passed in 1957, with 50-50 federal-provincial funding, and all provinces had put it into effect by 1961.

In the same year, Saskatchewan inaugurated a medical services plan, but it did not take full effect until more than a year later, after the government bowed to a physicians' strike and modified its mode of payment more to the doctors' liking. It seems to be true in all democracies that physician associations are able to hold governments hostage as an effective way of winning concessions.

The Canadian Medical Association (CMA) then made a fatal mistake. Alarmed by Saskatchewan's action, it asked for a national commission inquiry into health needs and health insurance. Its request backfired: The report issued in 1946 found that after 25 years of voluntary private insurance efforts almost half the population was uninsured. It concluded, to the utter dismay of the physicians, that "Canada requires the establishment of health insurance funds, provincially administered" and jointly financed.[3] The CMA's blunder and its effect on the legislative bargaining process were strikingly similar to the way in which the AMA's insistence that no more than a minimum be done in government-financed health care for the aged poor backfired and helped produce the combination of Medicare and Medicaid in the same year. In 1966, the medical program passed the Parliament, and by 1971 all provinces were participating.

Physicians were predictably unhappy with provincial efforts to hold down medical fees, and a new round of conflict and bargaining began over the issue of extra-billing—charging the patient more than the publicly paid fee. (Under Medicare in the United States, extra-billing is called balance billing and has been sharply limited in recent years.) A 1979 report urged a ban, which was instituted in 1984 (along with a ban on user charges, such as copayments) in the Canada Health Act. This law also, and more fundamentally, enunciated five principles that govern federal contributions to the jointly financed federal-state system. (The single-payer label on the Canadian system applies not to funding of the system but to the provider payments made by each province.)

Each province is constitutionally responsible for organizing the delivery system in its area, and to gain federal funding, each must do so in accord with the following five principles:

1. Comprehensiveness: Requires coverage of all medically necessary health services provided by hospitals and medical practitioners. (Coverage for dentistry, drugs, and long-term care are provided by the provinces, separately from the basic system, at varying levels.)
2. Universality: Requires that 100 percent of the population be insured for health services under uniform terms and conditions.
3. Portability: Requires that coverage continue as a person moves from one province to another.
4. Public administration: Requires that administration be by a public nonprofit authority, subject to audit, and responsible to the provincial government.
5. Accessibility: Requires reasonable access to insured health services unimpeded either directly or indirectly by charges or other means.

With a well-developed health services system, Canada enjoys good health statistics at substantially lower cost than in the United States. A dilemma of higher cost or lessened expectations is developing, however, as financial pressures of the late 1990s threaten the provinces' ability to live up to these principles.

Affordability Becomes an Issue

Canada's universal health care system had barely gotten underway when financial problems arose. By 1980 the national government gave itself some financial predictability by limiting annual increases in its health grants to the rate of growth in GNP, minus 3 percent. Expenditure increases beyond that became the full responsibility of each province. By 1995, the federal share had decreased to 32.9 percent of total provincial health care outlays. Reducing the federal government's contributions to the system did not, however, reduce costs for the whole system; it only shifted them to the provinces. And since 1990 there has been a "stampede to expenditure controls," precipitated by slow economic growth and the decline in federal subsidies.[4] The provinces took several steps to reduce expenditures: They set firm expenditure caps on physicians, as groups and even individually in some provinces; they reshaped programs through regionalization and limitations on capacity and manpower; and they improved operational efficiencies. These steps have been successful. Expenditures per capita have increased less than 1 percent annually since 1993 and have been reduced from 10.2 percent of GDP in 1992 to an estimated 9.2 percent in 1997.[5] Graphically, per capita cost is a flat line, and GDP share has a downward slope.

Financial pressures have been further increased by a 1996 statute that lumped Ottawa's contributions to health, postsecondary education, and social assistance programs into a single block grant, making it difficult to track the share that each province uses for health. Cost control efforts have been so bothersome to physicians that provinces have established a politically interesting new quasi-corporatist feature: comanagement committees for jointly monitoring fee limits and jointly considering policy issues raised by the income caps. Those committees represent a degree of cooperation between government and a group whose incomes the government wants to reduce that would not fit the U.S. political culture.

Whether the provinces would be able to continue adhering in good faith to the five principles—especially accessibility and comprehensiveness—began to seem questionable by 1996. In a less-than-vibrant economy, reductions in federal funding were not being fully made up by the provinces, and the public component of total national health expenditures fell to 68.7 percent by 1997. The obverse, of course, is that 31.3 percent, nearly a third, of Canadian health care expenditure is in the private sector—a fact as surprising as that nearly half of U.S. health expenditure is in the public sector.

A very substantial reduction (30 percent from 1987 to 1995) in active hospital beds was accompanied by earlier patient discharges, which meant increased private costs for pharmaceuticals, physiotherapists, and dressings at home. These kinds of steps were referred to by the Canadian Medical Association as "passive privatization."

Because the "medically necessary" services have nowhere been defined concretely, some provincial budget cuts in the 1990s have been in the form of "delisting" some services, thus switching costs for some treatments to the patient. Ontario, for instance, has delisted wart removals, reversal of vasectomies, and tubal ligations. In 1998 it issued a general policy statement specifying outdated and unproven procedures and solely cosmetic procedures as categories to be reviewed and circumscribed. At the western end of the country, British Columbia delisted cosmetic surgery, most dental services, and physical examinations required for employment, life insurance, educational enrollment, and so on. Delisting will not be favored by patients but has some attraction both for the provinces that pay all bills for covered treatments and for physicians who can charge separately for services that have been delisted.[6]

Any substantial move in this direction would, however, surely run afoul of the Canada Health Act principles, and Ottawa might cut payments to a province that delists what the national government deems to be medically necessary services or that adds user charges contravening the act. Indeed, passage of the act in 1984 with a proviso that *all* national grants-in-aid to the provinces—not just those for health—would be subject to withholding if the act was violated has been characterized as a recognition of overwhelming support for the health system. Continuing very strong political support in the national electorate for the five principles may today constitute the strongest lever against major loss of accessibility and coverage. As a deputy health minister put it in a speech, Canadians still "like the idea of living in a country where they don't check your credit rating before they check your pulse."[7]

Perhaps it was a case of darkest before dawn. By the spring of 1998, a brighter range of possibilities was beginning to emerge. Canada's economic growth rate was thought likely to be the highest among G-7 nations that year. The federal budget came into balance, and the Minister of Health declared that the era of health care budget cuts was over. If so, many doubtless felt it was just in time. Even close Canadian observers disagree on what the future holds. Budgets may improve but continue to be tight. Physician groups are unhappy, many even bitter, about tight fee caps. Yet the public wants to expand the system to include pharmaceuticals and long-term care, and the government is taking those desires seriously in its announced planning efforts. (These services are currently provided at varying levels by provinces, especially for the elderly, and by larger employers.)

To its American would-be copiers, Canadian health care looks like an inviting model for low-cost, high-quality service delivery. Among Canadian stakeholders, public and private, it is a fine system but seen to be under great stress. Cost control and the proper range of health services are a major issue north as well as south of the U.S.-Canadian border.

United Kingdom: Socialism with Private Beds

Britain (the United Kingdom is the official name for the country comprising England, Scotland, Wales, and Northern Ireland, but Great Britain is often used as a synonym) is a unitary rather than a federal governmental system. In consequence, it has a more centralized overall framework for its health care. The National Health Service of the United Kingdom is the most socialized, in the institutional sense, of the three systems sketched here. As part of its legislative formation, the hospitals were nationalized and the specialists (called "consultants") based in them became government salaried. Primary care physicians (general practitioners) receive capitation payments from a regional public authority as independent contractors, but they also receive office and staff subsidies and are in the NHS superannuation (retirement) plan. Because it covers the entire population in a single health care delivery system and is financed almost entirely by the national government, NHS's global budget provides stronger leverage for rational health care planning than is found in other countries.

Overall priorities are set in the use of major categories of resources, including, for example, locating physicians in areas of need, seeing that the geriatric specialty has some priority in medical education as the population ages, limiting the proliferation of expensive equipment, and gearing services to the major demographic variables in each region. Because health services are only 6.9 percent of GDP in Britain and it has only 1.6 physicians per thousand population (Germany has 3.3), careful use of funds and staff is imperative; central budget control makes it possible.

At the same time, there is a substantial private element in British health care. Each hospital has "private pay" beds in which patients having supplementary private insurance are treated by specialists in what we might call a "moonlighting" arrangement. Privately insured patients can jump the queue, or waiting list, for operations such as hip replacements. This situation has stimulated private insurance, which about 10 percent of the population now hold, using it mostly as a hospitalization supplement to their NHS coverage.[8] One study estimates that 20 percent of operations are privately paid for.[9]

An interesting difference between Britain and Canada is that the latter's law does not permit doctors to offer privately any services covered by the national health insurance system—although this practice is allowed in the otherwise more socialized United Kingdom. In Canada, a physician who wants a private practice must opt out and not have any publicly insured patients. There are therefore very few private practices in Canada. The special egalitarian thrust of the Canadian system is well illustrated in a commentary on this difference from a noted economist-observer in Canada:

> The British private consultant [specialist] . . . can use his position within the NHS to manipulate waiting lists and other aspects of access so as to ensure that private

care will be preferable to those who can afford it. The Canadian physician who decides to "go private" must go all the way. He cannot use a strategic position with the
public system to cream off only the profitable patients for his private services.[10]

Is cost control too strong if it results in long waits for nonemergency treatment? Waiting lists for nonemergency surgical procedures are common in a
number of countries. In Britain, they are considered a trade-off for ensuring
that everyone has access to care while keeping costs considerably lower than in
Canada, Germany, or the United States. The number of people on the queue is
not really as important as the length of the wait, but the former causes the
greater political embarrassment. As of early 1997, the waiting lists for hospitalization in England totaled one and a half million people, although the average
waiting time of 13 or 14 months has been constant since the 1960s. Having
queues sounds outrageous to Americans. But to the British, having 16 or 17
percent of the population entirely without any insured right to care—and
therefore not eligible even to get on the waiting list for nonemergency treatment—is at least equally outrageous. Each is a form of rationing in the sense of
distributing scarce resources. Is one clearly better than the other?

Building Coverage from the Bottom Up

Great Britain had private sickness clubs and "friendly societies" through which
blue-collar workers might obtain medical assistance before the National Insurance Act of 1911 used these as the instruments through which to fund a free
general practitioner service. The uniform minimum plan did not include hospitalization or treatment by specialists, although some local societies did provide hospital care and dentistry. Twelve million workers, but no dependents,
were covered initially. For wives (even for maternity care) and children of
workers and the middle class, private insurance had to supplement what the
workers received. The very poor might get treatment through a free hospital
outpatient clinic. In the early 1920s, people of low income were able to buy insurance for treatment in voluntary (community) hospitals, and some large
employers paid for all their low-pay workers.

When World War II began, half the adults were still outside the system, and
hospital benefits remained what the British call a "hotch-potch" affair. Only
the very poor were sure of hospital care in a system where others feared having
to spend down into poverty before they would be treated. From an American
point of view, this care for the very poor was an early equivalent to Medicaid—

except that the U.S. national program for the poor came into being *after* the middle and upper classes had obtained private coverage, not before. In both Germany and Britain, one sees an element of noblesse oblige, a social solidarity heritage of feudal times when lords of the manor were owed allegiance by their serfs and in return felt responsible for them. A very different social basis from the American emphasis on individual liberty and individual responsibility.

Inter-war (1918–1939) surveys had shown an appalling need for better health care—and nutrition and housing, too. In 1942, the famed Beveridge Report on postwar social insurance goals gave a clarion call for major change. When the Labour Party, favoring government ownership of essential industries and services, took over from Churchill's Conservative government in the first postwar election, the time was ripe for the creation of the National Health Service. Nationalization of most hospitals was part of the plan, along with universal coverage, no longer limited to lower income workers. As in the United States—and despite the strong parliamentary form of government in which the executive leader, the prime minister, comes out of the majority party's contingent in the House of Commons—much compromising with interest groups was involved. The British Medical Association chairman told the Minister of Health at one point, "We have the doctors; you want the doctors." As when Medicare passed Congress, the government had to make concessions to the organized physicians for fear they might go on strike. The physicians got a right to continue taking private patients, and they got private pay beds for them in public hospitals. They also got a strong corporatist voice in the operation of the system in the form of a substantial proportion of seats on hospital boards and executive councils. (An interesting partial counterpart is the Medicare Payment Advisory Commission. Established by Congress, it gives advice that the legislators follow rather closely regarding DRG rates for hospitals and the fee schedule for physicians. Membership includes prominent physicians, medical center and managed care executives, and an AFL-CIO representative.)

The NHS is a strong, respected universal health service run by a democratic government (in a constitutional monarchy). It has an especially strong reputation for emergency care and for treatment of pregnant women and young children, and it is ahead of the United States in developing a cadre of geriatricians. But it did not arise overnight. The change from limited, publicly funded insurance for blue collar workers to universal coverage through a governmentally operated delivery system took nearly half a century, and it took a couple of decades more to become a planned structure with a major program to replace hospitals built in Victorian days—a process not yet completed.

A Very Tight Lid on Costs

In Britain, where nationally allocated public funds account for 95 percent of NHS, with minor user charges for the rest, costs over the years have been the lowest per capita and as a percent of GDP among industrial nations. Greater efficiency has been sought in recent years. Some of Prime Minister Margaret Thatcher's Conservative party wanted to privatize health care, but she did not try to go that far. With a close to messianic sense of a mission to marketize Britain's entire mode of operation, she did institute a system of "internal markets," which meant separating purchasers from providers. Instead of each hospital having a budget directly from central government authority, the funds were placed in the hands of district authorities to contract with hospitals (publicly owned by substantially autonomous "trusts") and physicians. Practitioners get some of their income on a capitation basis and some from fees for screening exams, immunizations, and similar services.

Just before the Labour party took over in the spring of 1997, the system was reported to be deteriorating. There was talk of a dilemma: raising taxes (no more popular there than in the United States) or applying substantial user charges (which would undermine the tradition of the National Health Service). Reducing the scope of covered services was also mentioned.[11] Some experts say that operations of dubious value, like tonsillectomies, should be restricted, and it has been argued that infertility treatments and removal of nonpainful varicose veins do not involve healing the sick and therefore should not be part of NHS coverage. Some regional authorities already exclude tattoo removal, vasectomies, and sterilization operations.

Prime Minister Tony Blair's Labour government had rhetorically castigated the internal market during the 1997 election campaign but is keeping the separation of buyers of treatments from the sellers. Instead of doing so in the name of competition, however, the focus is to be on cooperation: working out three-year purchaser-provider agreements for health services in each region. The Labour government is moving to create large primary care groups (the specialists are hospital based), some 500 of them, each to serve a geographic population of 100,000 people. They will be responsible to the regional health authorities, which will in turn be responsible to the central government. The net effect of the organizational changes will be to centralize the system after what had been a period of decentralization.[12]

The NHS is the pride of the Labour party, and the crowning achievement of Britain's welfare state. The social-economic thrust of the system is evident in the comment of the director of an emergency department in a London hospital: "In the United States, if you fall over, they frisk you for your Blue Cross care before they take you to hospital, but here, everybody gets treated, even the scruffiest drunk."[13] That's one side of the picture. The other shows the tightest cost control among major nations. It is a point of envy at times, but the question at the end of the 1990s is whether the budget had become too tight. The Blair government apparently thinks so itself, for in July 1998 it announced a 50th anniversary "present" for the NHS: a three-year health budget of 21 billion pounds, estimated to produce an above-inflation increase of 4.75 percent a year.[14]

Germany: Public Framework, Private Operation

Although Canada is the (mostly) English-speaking neighbor of the United States and they share both television programs and auto manufacturing companies, Germany's health care system more closely resembles that of the United States in the extent of private funding and private operation. It is publicly established, however, and operates within nationally legislated budgetary limits.

Coverage in the German system is very good: Sickness fund benefits include physician and hospital care, preventive measures and screening, substantial dental benefits, and a very strong pharmaceutical program. Recently, sickness funds have begun competing for subscribers, so some have offered such benefits as yoga, diet consultation, and exercise classes—something like HMO competition in the United States. Maternity benefits include a worker's income replacement while on leave, household assistance, and cash allowances for children in the first year. Copayments are small. The broad social insurance system includes the sickness funds, accident insurance, pension funds, and unemployment insurance. Surprisingly, in the face of rising cost problems (see below), in 1995 Germany mandated an extensive home health and nursing home program for the elderly, to be paid for by employers and employees each contributing 1 percent of payroll. (Employer opposition was overcome by canceling one paid holiday.)

By national law, all workers with earnings under about $44,000 (1997 figure)—which means about 92 percent of workers—must belong to the system.[15] Higher income persons may opt out with private insurance (and a substantial number of those in the official system also buy supplementary coverage, such as for a single or double hospital room rather than a four-person ward). Instead of taxpayer support and a government agency to dole out the money to providers, however, the law mandates that employers and employees support health care services by funding nonprofit insurance organizations known as "sickness funds," which began as something like worker cooperatives in the nineteenth century.[16] These funds annually estimate their needs, then impose levies (which Americans might think of as private taxes) on employers and employees to raise the money. The funds then negotiate with physician associations, which in turn disburse the money to individual doctors in accord with a fee schedule. Every employer and employee must pay into the system on a 50-50 basis, at the established rate, the combined level of which presently averages about 13 percent of wages. There are many detailed complexities, but that's the nub of the matter. In being financed entirely through employer-employee contributions to nonprofit organizations, the system is more private than Medicare and Medicaid; in its compulsory membership and governmentally established policy framework, it is much more public-sector oriented than the overall system in the United States. And in its heavy reliance on organized private groups for its operation, it is uniquely corporatist among the nations covered here.

Corporatism is a significant aspect of the German and Japanese political economies, denoting a close working relationship between private organizations and the national government. I am not using "corporatism" as a euphemism for interest group pressures on a legislator or for lobbyists sitting in on drafting legislation, as does happen in the United States. Rather, I am referring to an arrangement of mutual dependence and obligation. Americans have the dependence: Government officials often, properly and usefully, obtain information and policy ideas from representatives of interest groups; but Americans lack the mutual obligation. In the United States, each group is expected to seek the best deal it can for itself, without great regard for the good of the commons (i.e., the whole community, the whole nation), and an obligation to government in exchange for some benefit is not often part of the bargain. In Germany, the national government has granted great authority to private bodies, but in return they accept that they must stay within the bargains set. For an important example, German law protects workers from rapid health care inflation by requiring that annual contributions not rise by more than average worker compensation. The insurers and the providers are not free to raise rates as an American insurer or HMO may as a matter of private business discretion. Group discipline, not devil-take-the-hindmost individualism, is a hallmark of the German political system—in many areas, not just in health care.

From Medieval Guilds, a Corporatist System

Germany was the first nation to institute a mandated health insurance system. Even before Germany became a unified nation, the King of Prussia had established in 1854 the first compulsory sickness fund system for foundries and mines. In 1883, Chancellor Bismarck gave to the sickness funds, which had grown out of medieval craftsmen guilds, responsibility for the health care of workers in blue-collar industrial occupations. Coverage was gradually extended to other groups: agricultural workers in 1911; the unemployed in 1918; seamen in 1927; pensioners in 1941; salesmen in 1966; self-employed agricultural workers and dependents in 1975; and students and the disabled in 1975.

Ambulatory physician associations are powerful group negotiators, with official status (which is a hallmark of corporatism). There are 960 funds—almost as cumbersome as the plenitude of insurance plans in the United States.[17] They are not consolidated because worker loyalties to their particular funds are so strong it would be too risky politically to insist on rationalizing the structure, which shows that even a very strong parliamentary government must watch its step with the voters.

Payroll deductions are based on ability to pay, reflecting the general European social ethic that health care is a part of the "cement that binds a people sharing the same geography into a genuine nation," as health economist Uwe Reinhardt has written.[18] Every German enjoys one amenity that many Americans might envy: being sent to a spa for three weeks of mineral baths and massages to ameliorate arthritis or as a "mother recovery cure" after a woman gives birth. Baden-Baden for the masses!

Cost Control through Corporatist Cooperation

Germany's health care system has been no more immune to financial challenges and change in the 1980s and 1990s than the system in the United States. A sensed need to strengthen cost controls came in part because of the inevitable slowing down of the economic growth rate associated with the "German miracle" of the early postwar years. Unification with much poorer East Germany added severe financial strains as the 1980s ended, and health care was one of the areas looked to for savings. Success in holding down health care's share of GDP is a major reason why American health care policy makers are close observers of Germany. But good controls did not come overnight.

An organization called Concerted Action was formed in 1977. With 70 representatives of stakeholder interests, it set guidelines periodically for cost trends, advised by a strong set of experts. The sickness funds used these guidelines in negotiating with provider groups, such as the National Association of Sickness Fund Physicians. A relative value scale was used, and the annual conversion factor to translate the point rating of a fee into money was negotiated. This system controlled prices but not the volume of services, so in 1986 the funds switched to negotiating an annual global sum for each region. If the physicians do more than expected, the payment per service is reduced. Note that this method creates a strong incentive for doctors to agree to reviewing what they all do.

In 1992, another large area of increasing cost was attacked: prescription medications. Until then, price controls had been placed only on pharmacists' markups, not on the manufacturers, and their prices were very high. The new law cut some prices and then froze producer prices for three years, and drug price controls continue, set by classes of drugs. To counter a medical and popular culture that encouraged heavy use of pharmaceuticals, the government has also instituted drug budgets for physicians, who must pay a portion of costs for prescribing over the budgeted limits. These new controls were part of a Structural Health Reform Act that preempted the Concerted Action negotiations with a freeze on sickness fund contribution rates and set hard annual budget targets for hospitals. As part of a political bargain, it acknowledged that the doctors had done their share and it was time for other health sectors to feel the heat of cost control.

Strongly disciplined parties in a strong parliamentary system are a major political factor enabling Germany to impose both price and volume controls on medical providers, specifically physicians and pharmaceutical suppliers. The first expenditure reform steps were taken in 1987, limiting the amount that sickness funds could negotiate with physician associations to the growth rate of fund members' income. The corporatist pattern of agreed limits apparently worked well: In the 1980s, when U.S. health expenditures rose 33 percent higher each year than the GDP growth rate, Germany's health rate increased only 3 percent more than GDP.

Stability in the payroll deduction compelled stability in physician compensation rates. A schedule of charges rather like the U.S. relative value scale in Medicare was used to set fee-for-service payments that were supposed not to exceed, in total, the money that the payroll deduction would generate in a given year. A major effort to control the volume of services as well as the price came with legislation passed at the end of 1992. (Every nation has found that price controls alone lead to providers delivering more services, to maintain personal income targets.) DRGs for hospital procedures have been introduced, again following U.S. experience.

In contrast to these regulatory price controls over hospitals, physicians, and pharmaceuticals, Germany has also introduced some market competition, primarily by allowing free choice of sickness funds for the first time. As sickness fund premiums sometimes have differed substantially, this change may be a significant market-oriented step in a system that has overwhelmingly embodied the principle of social solidarity rather than of individualism.

The politics of use review has an interesting German difference from the United States. Known as "economic monitoring," it involves a committee of representatives of both the funds and the physician association comparing a doctor's level of services with the norm for his or her specialty. If services are done at a rate more than 25 percent above the norm the provider may have to return funds to the association. Individual incomes are thus subordinated to the requirements of the group, and laymen (from the sickness funds) sit equally with physicians in the monitoring committees.

Despite a so-far effective cost control pattern, German stability in health care finance faces additional, predictable challenges for the future. The population is aging and will need more medical services, while the proportion of working age people is declining. By the year 2030, 37 percent of the population of the former West Germany will be over 60. Limiting the pool of funds to a fixed rate of employer-employee contributions will clearly be strained. As funding problems are anticipated, different models for a tightened system are being discussed. The basic principle underlying scenarios proposed by the Advisory Council of the Ministry of Health would divide the benefits between core and optional sections, with an opportunity to opt out and use private insurance for the noncore benefits. It is apparently thought that the past success of cost restraint measures cannot be matched in the future without very substantial changes in the benefit package.

To Each Its Own

We have seen that medical cultures vary from country to country, even though the biomedical knowledge base is essentially the same for all of them. It should therefore not surprise us that the organization and financing of health care systems also vary—and vary considerably.

Given the American predilection for viewing all politico-economic questions through thick ideological glasses, whether conservative or liberal, perhaps the most striking finding of our quick review of how the others do it is the considerable mixture of private and public, national and regional elements in each of the nations covered. The most institutionally socialized, the United Kingdom, reserves beds for private patients in nationalized hospitals. The mostly privately organized, Germany, has a strong base in compulsory national legislation, though the system operates in quite decentralized fashion.

Some advocates for change seem to assume, with unnecessary envy, that universal health insurance was achieved all at once in other countries. That, we have seen, has hardly been the case. It has been a struggle everywhere—though the others have reached the universal coverage goal line ahead of Americans. Although it is true that the United States has far and away the highest cost system, none of the others has satisfactorily solved the problem of steadily increasing costs either. We're all in the same boat: Can we meet our populations' medical expectations without far exceeding their willingness to pay, privately or publicly?

Overall, our quick survey confirms John Iglehart's observation that all health care systems have "features arrived at through historical accident, cultural preference, and political compromise that make little sense today."

7

Managed Care

Boon or Bane? Both!

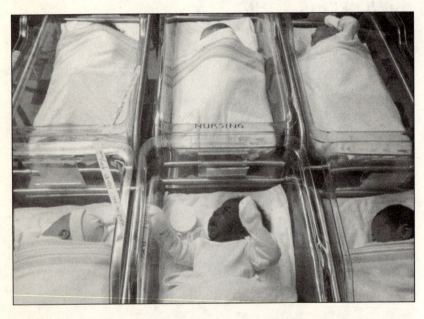

Medicine, pre- and post-nurseries. Photo courtesy of Stock Boston, © Herb Snitzer, reprinted with permission.

Aɴ Aᴜɢᴜsᴛ 1997 Kᴀɪsᴇʀ/Hᴀʀᴠᴀʀᴅ national survey found that 51 percent of the people responding believed that managed care has decreased the quality of care for sick people (32 percent said increased).[1] In another 1997 survey, in California, 42 percent of respondents said that they had experienced a problem with their health plan, and 21 percent of these asserted that their problem involved actions that had led to worsening of their condition.[2] Patients give contradictory reports in surveys, with 79 percent in one 1996 survey agreeing with a statement that "there is something seriously wrong with our health care system," yet 57 percent in the same survey agreed that "my medical plan provides me the best quality care I could want."[3] A recent careful analysis of many surveys of public reactions to managed care concludes that the backlash is being driven by two major factors, the first being that a substantial portion of enrollees report problems with their plans. The second is "relatively rare events that seem threatening and dramatic but have been experienced by few consumers personally," like reports of a child's cancer treatment being held back.[4]

Physicians have apparently been no happier than patients: Over half of doctors responding to a 1995 survey said that the health system was deteriorating, especially in areas served by managed care providers.

What's the true story? Are HMOs, PPOs, POSs—the whole array of organized health plans with varying degrees of restriction on patient choice of physicians—a good thing or a bad thing? What are the pros and cons? And how is public policy being shaped by the experiences and fears of voter-members of managed care health plans, the lobbying of health care organizations, and the media's "feeding frenzy" over every new anecdote about a patient disabled or dying because of a treatment denied?

Is the choice facing Americans either:

1. prohibitively expensive traditional fee-for-service medicine provided through a "cottage industry" of individual practitioners, whom one can freely choose from among those whose fees one can afford and who can increase their incomes by telling patients they need more tests and more medical services, or

2. lower costs (for one's own care and for the share each taxpayer contributes to Medicare and Medicaid) by limiting one's choice of physician, who will be paid a flat per-person fee that may discourage her from providing any test or service not clearly required or from referring one to a specialist?

That's one oversimplified way of expressing the managed care dilemma as currently viewed through a jaundiced media eye. Another way focuses on the push toward a set of explicit consumer protections—such as a right to sue managed care companies, to establish independent appeals processes, and to be informed of a health plan's financial arrangements with its practitioners. A spokesperson for the American Association of Health Plans reacted to these ideas: "Is this going to improve quality or is it going to micromanage plans, drive health costs up and leave fewer people with insurance?"

Given the controversy in which managed care in general and HMOs in particular are enveloped, we need to examine the pros and cons as policy makers face them. To do that we first need to sketch the landscape.

A Managed Care Profile

The concept associated with the acronym HMO (for health maintenance organization) far antedates its name. The idea of an organization that would combine insurance and the provision of a full range of medical services for a fixed monthly fee has been an institutional reality since Henry J. Kaiser created in the 1930s what is now known as Kaiser Permanente to meet the needs of employees in an isolated location. Expanded during World War II when Kaiser became a major West Coast shipbuilder, it then took on a life of its own.

(Although Kaiser Permanente is the modern prototype, similar ways of providing health care to a defined group had existed much earlier. Some early manufacturing and mining firms hired physicians and nurses to care for workers in company towns. Company doctors were part of what has been called the United Mine Workers' "noble experiment."[5] Much further back, guilds of craftsmen and miners in the medieval German states were offered sick pay in return for annual fixed contributions—capitation fees—that were usually paid to sickness funds in installments on feast days of patron saints. In the nineteenth century, sickness funds hired doctors on a salary or capitation basis, and workers using out-of-plan doctors had to pay wholly out-of-pocket. Perhaps the earliest health insurance, not of an HMO type, was in ancient China, where one paid a doctor while healthy and suspended payments when one became sick!)

Preventive services and continuity of care are the putative distinguishing characteristics of HMOs, and this emphasis on *maintaining* health and minimizing the need for acute care is the reason Dr. Paul Ellwood created the health maintenance organization label as a symbol for this break from traditional medicine. He was consulted by President Nixon's health policy advisers, who felt a need for a health care initiative to counter a 1970 threat that Senator Edward M. Kennedy might push national health insurance through the Democratic Congress. The Nixon administration adopted both the HMO strategy and Ellwood's label.[6] "Health maintenance" is a positive sounding phrase and has presumably aided acceptance of the new form of health care delivery.

An important conceptual distinction among HMOs is their degree of integration. Staff and group models either have salaried employees or contract with large medical groups to provide a range of services; some, like Kaiser, have their own hospitals as well. Much looser are network-based plans, in which a health plan management contracts with several provider groups, and independent practice associations (IPAs), in which an insurer or other managing entity contracts with individual physicians who continue to operate their own offices and see nonplan patients on an FFS basis. Solo doctors often sign up with a number of health plans simultaneously. (The varying regulations of each plan are a major reason why physicians in independent practice complain so much about the excessive cost and annoyance of having to hire extra office staff to keep up with the rules and the paperwork requirements of different plans).

One further difference among HMOs should be noted: profit or nonprofit status. Kaiser, the largest of all HMOs with 9 million subscribers, is nonprofit, as are two other long-time HMOs: Health Insurance Plan of New York and Group Health Cooperative of Puget Sound, in Washington state. The growth surge has, however, been of for-profit firms, which now constitute nearly three-fourths of all HMO plans. In 1981, only 12 percent of HMO subscribers were in for-profit plans; that figure is now about 62 percent.[7] The for-profit health plans are overwhelmingly publicly traded, investor-owned entities from which Wall Street expects (though it does not always obtain) continuous profit growth. This aspect of today's managed care universe plays no small part in the backlash against HMOs, as both physicians and patients fear that the drive for profit will lead to cutting corners on delivery of care and quality of care.

Ironically, just as HMOs seemed to have become the dominant player in employers' quest for the holy grail of cost reduction, competition among them for subscribers began to dilute their most basic cost-saving strategy: using a closed panel of physicians. As I write, anecdotal evidence (the picture changes faster than annual surveys can keep up) indicates that the new hot "product" is the point of service (POS) plan. The name suggests its rationale: At the point of needing care, the subscriber decides whether to use the plan provider or an outsider at a higher copay. In other words, POS plans are HMO-PPO hybrids.

As these variations imply, the clear distinctions among HMO types are disappearing as a consequence of competition for subscribers (which makes it difficult to have completely accurate figures on trends). The largest national plans offer both pure HMOs (i.e., a fixed panel of providers) and looser plans, so that employers have a range of types and prices from which to choose. The essence of all, however, is that the bulk of care is provided through an organization receiving a fixed monthly sum for each enrollee.

HMO enrollments (all types) were 2.9 million in 1970, were 9 million by 1980, and had tripled again to a subscriber base of 34.7 million by 1990—a clear reflection of mounting employer-purchaser efforts to trim health benefits costs. In less than a decade, enrollment doubled from that point to 76 million subscribers as 1998 began. Evidence of the popularity of the open-ended versions of HMOs is their enrollment increase from 1 million in 1990 to 12 million as of January 1998. Total managed care enrollment (HMOs, PPOs, POS plans, etc.) may reach 100 million by the year 2000. Traditional FFS plans are fast becoming dodo birds. Interestingly, the number of HMO organizations has had relatively little net growth: 556 plans in 1990 and 651 as of January 1998. Consolidation, especially strong at the end of the decade, explains why the growth of plans has not been greater: Larger, national plans that can service national employers at multiple locations have a competitive advantage. Despite the plethora of marketing-induced variations among plans, 85 percent of total HMO enrollment is in the basic, fixed-panel of providers plans.[8]

Managed care has some additional forms that do not fit any of the HMO forms. One is the preferred provider organization (PPO), which simply means a list of doctors or hospitals who are "preferred" because they offer discounted fees to subscribers. A higher copayment is required if the subscriber insists on using a nonplan provider. There are also exclusive provider organizations (EPOs), which compel the subscriber to see a provider on the discount list or pay the entire bill himself. And the latest contenders for employer contracts are provider sponsored organizations (PSOs). The concept is that physicians and hospitals band together as their own HMOs to eliminate the insurer "middleman." Financial strength and management questions may limit their growth, but it is too early to tell.

Even some FFS plans are included in the managed care category, because they almost all use preadmission hospital clearance, second opinions, discharge planning, and other utilization rules. However, I do not focus on them here because they do not operate by fixed subscriber premiums or capitation of providers and thus do not involve the crucial reversal of incentives faced by providers in HMOs and related forms.

In the early IPAs, the independent physician was often paid on a fee-for-service basis but at a discounted rate from his normal charge. The health plan as a whole was then the financially at-risk party. Hospitals receiving per diems were in a similar situation. Now hospitals are often receiving fixed payments for a given condition (like Medicare DRGs), and capitation has become the modal form by which HMOs pay the medical groups who do the actual care. (Capitation sometimes includes withholding and bonus complexities; see below.) Much of the financial risk in providing care is thus being transferred from HMO management to the constituent providers.

There has been a strong geographic concentration of HMOs: As of 1995, 16 states had over 20 percent of their population in HMOs, whereas in 20 states the figure was less than 10 percent. Oregon (with 42 percent) and Massachusetts (with 39.9 percent) had the highest percentages, totaling 3.7 million people, but California's 37.6 percent accounted for 12.2 million people—almost a fourth of the national total. However, a more even geographic distribution will be a natural side effect of more and more companies choosing managed care for their employees, and Medicare has increased rates to rural plans, which will stimulate more efforts to enroll seniors in more areas.

There is a considerable and growing concentration of size: Of 630 HMOs in January 1996, the 25 largest held 35.5 percent of pure HMO enrollment, and the largest 25 offering the POS option held 62.4 percent of the enrollment in that hybrid form. Nearly half of total managed care enrollment is accounted for by the 7 largest national firms. In California, mergers have left just 3 firms covering 9 out of 13 million HMO subscribers.[9]

Public policy has encouraged HMO competition as the way to lower costs and improve quality, but where the competition is so strong that smaller firms are swallowed up by a few giants, some think that a resulting oligopolistic pattern will undermine the competitive principle. Conversely, integration into a small number of very large organizations creates a more centralized health care delivery system overall, which means both stronger opportunities for developing health strategies for large populations and a more manageable regulatory universe for governmental health planning.

Medicare enrollment in HMOs has been much slower to take hold than among below-65 persons. From 1985 to 1990 Medicare HMO enrollment increased only from 0.8 to 1.5 million people and then to 3.1 million in 1995. Seniors are more likely to have established relationships with physicians, often for treatment of a chronic condition, and are loath to change doctors. They also may find it harder to navigate the bureaucracy of large organizations after being accustomed to the small office of a solo practitioner for many years. In the late 1990s, however, they began to move to managed care in greater numbers, with HCFA reporting 5.6 million Medicare enrollees (15 percent of the senior population) in managed care as of September 1997. The strongest reason was probably the extra benefits offered by many HMOs, especially prescription drugs at very low cost, plus eye exams and glasses. Another reason lies in the substantial upward price increase in supplementary (Medigap) policies in 1997, encouraging more seniors to join plans that would eliminate or reduce deductibles and copayments. Legislation in 1997 enlarging seniors' options to include senior PPO and POS plans is expected to draw in more subscribers—if they are not totally confused by the complex menu of offerings. Of course, the federal and state governments hope that the public sector's rate of health care cost increase—8.7 percent versus 2.9 for the private sector in 1995—will drop as Medicare and Medicaid patients enroll in managed care plans.

Between 1994 and 1996 competition for market share brought price increases to purchasers to a near halt—even a slight decline in premiums in 1994—while costs of serving subscribers kept climbing. The change in premium pattern was striking and sudden. Health benefit cost increases to employers had ranged from 8 percent in the year just preceding the decrease up to the 17–19 percent range in 1988–1990. When price increases hit bottom as the fight for market share heated up, 40 percent of HMOs reported operating losses in 1995. By 1997–1998 the trend of prices was on the way up again as companies concentrated on improving their own financial health. Reduction in the number of major competitors may aid the survivors in doing so.

Ways of trying to save money sometimes change the way medicine is practiced—and not always for the worse. Mental health care has often been "carved out" by an HMO, contracting for such care to be handled by a separate, specialized behavioral health organization. A chain of cancer treatment groups is arranging nationwide contracts with HMOs. Case managers are often appointed for close supervision of chronic condition cases, such as diabetes and asthma, helping to ensure continuity of care. In many such arrangements, the payment mode usually remains fee-for-service. Oxford Health Plans took a bold step in 1997 by arranging for hundreds of specialists to handle treatment of various procedures, like heart bypass operations, breast cancer, and hip replacements, on a "global fee" basis. That is, instead of being paid on a FFS basis and having to seek approval at each stage of an expensive course of treatment, the physicians are paid an all-inclusive price for a single "episode of care," based on experience with the components and time elements of a particular kind of treatment. Oxford expected to save about 15 percent over the FFS fees it had been paying.

For the specialists, the carrot in a deal that offers less money is a medically significant one: greater clinical autonomy. Because the doctors will not be able to demand more money for extra steps in a treatment plan, the health plan does not need to micromanage. It gets rid of one of the hated features of concurrent utilization review and provides greater respect for a doctor's professionalism. But just as no good deed goes unpunished, no innovation goes without criticism. In this case, a spokesperson for the New York State Medical Society feared that HMOs might contract on the basis of lowest bids rather than physicians' reputations for quality care. Time will tell. It is an interesting step in cost containment.

In summary, managed care is rapidly replacing traditional health insurance but with its exact forms still in a rapidly evolving state. The cost control objective held by employer-purchasers and HMO managers wars constantly with the subscriber-patients' strong desire for maximum choice. Where keen competition makes it hardest to raise prices, there is also the greatest pressure to accommodate the more costly POS option. It may take some time to reach a new equilibrium—if, indeed, one can be reached within the existing market system.

As of mid-1998, with Congress facing midterm elections and hundreds of bills in the hopper to respond to the clamor for regulating managed care in the name of "patients' rights," the battle over public policy was increasing in intensity. The recommendations of the Clinton Administration's Advisory Commission on Consumer Protection and Quality in the Health Care Industry stimulated considerable congressional dispute. Clinton put them into effect by executive order early in 1998 for 85 million people covered by federally administered health plans, and in June he ordered even more extensive and more specific patient protections for Medicare and Medicaid patients. For example, women may demand direct access to a women's health specialist for routine services like Pap smears and pelvic examinations, there are penalties for discriminating against sick or poor people in marketing efforts by the health plans, and health plans must respond appropriately to the needs of patients of diverse cultural backgrounds or limited English proficiency. Even without legislation, these administrative actions can have a considerable effect on the private sector. The battle lines had been drawn in fall 1997, when House Majority Leader Dick Armey charged that the commission's recommendations were a disguised effort to "nationalize health care" and the Republicans sent out letters to stimulate lobbyists to mount a campaign against what they pictured as a devious Clinton plan to bring his failed health reforms back to life via incremental regulations. The president seems to have conceded that point, saying that "almost the whole population wants to keep nibbling away at the apple until we actually have solved the problems of cost, accessibility and quality for all responsible American citizens."[10] Health care remains high on the political agenda and may well be a major issue in the 2000 presidential campaign.

The Case for Managed Care

Despite lower increases in health care premiums in recent years and the faith of employers that shifting their employees to managed care will save lots of money, the evidence so far is not clear. Critics contend that managed care does not save much money. For example, California, with very high HMO penetration, continues to have high per capita health expenditures; however, its rate of increase in recent years was far less then the national average. Critics also charge that managed care lowers quality by putting bottom line considerations ahead of doing everything that might benefit patients. Problem anecdotes abound and have created a backlash. One might well ask, Is there anything good to be said of HMOs?

The answer is clearly yes—in principle and at least some of the time in practice. Because many critics (perhaps especially older FFS practitioners and their older patients) tend to assume the worst kind of bottom-line oriented HMO as their model, fairness calls for ticking off managed care's potential advantages by assuming an HMO that embodies the best of the form.

We might start with a real (but not often recognized by the public) advantage of HMOs: absence of the FFS incentive to *overtreat*. When the physician's income increases by doing procedures and the insurance plan accepts without question what the doctor decides, there is no flag saying, "Let's stop and think about whether this procedure is really necessary or whether more conservative treatment might be worth trying first." Angioplasties, Cesarean sections, and the use of antibiotics for head colds have been overused in FFS practice, according to medical researchers. HMO protocols and gatekeeping requirements may avoid unnecessary operations. Also, as stockbrokers have been known to "churn the account" (i.e., recommend changes in holdings to increase transaction fees), physicians in FFS practice may be tempted to order more tests, require more visits, and do more procedures to maintain their "target income." Evidence that overtreating to generate income does happen is found in data showing an increase in the volume of services when a scale of lower fees is imposed on doctors. Among the serious yet not widely recognized problems of health care are iatrogenic (physician-induced) and nosocomial (hospital induced) infections and diseases. The more treatment given, the greater the number of such occurrences.

A major potential benefit—partly medical, partly economic—is comprehensiveness of care. Coordinated care in an integrated delivery system is a real advantage. When a single organization includes most of the specialties and even ancillary services (e.g., physical and occupational therapy, nutritional advice) of a modern medical armamentarium, the patient may be able to draw on members of a team who know each other (and each other's ways of thinking, strengths, and weaknesses). The team may all be knowledgeable about a patient's particular situation and thus be able to develop an optimal treatment plan. It is increasingly recognized that such a team is particularly important in handling chronic conditions, such as asthma and diabetes. A closely integrated delivery system is also likely to have a far better patient information system than looser arrangements like IPAs. In traditional practice, the information "system" consists of little more than patients informing their family physician of treatments done or medications prescribed by specialists visited without referral.

A large, strong health plan can take an approach centered on an entire population of enrollees, producing advantages for the subscriber group as a whole. Being in a global budget situation (its monthly premium times the number of subscribers gives it a known, fixed income), the HMO is encouraged to take the "maintenance" part of the acronym seriously (if it has a stable roster of subscribers) and engage in a kind of public health strategy. HMOs often offer services beyond those covered by many traditional insurance policies: vision and dental care, well baby clinics, immunizations, screenings for cancer or heart problems, fitness programs, and other preventive measures. A family practice doctor taking time (if his workload permits it!) to help a patient adopt a nonsmoking lifestyle, begin an aerobic fitness regime, or lose weight is building a healthier subscriber base. Because the HMO saves money when subscribers need fewer treatments, a healthier list of enrollees translates into a healthier bottom line for the health plan and (if it's for-profit) its investors. Both parties gain.

Closely related is managed care's emphasis on using primary care physicians to do much routine treatment that might otherwise be done by specialists. For the patient, communication with a single doctor visited for a variety of needs is very likely to be better than with a variety of doctors seen only occasionally. This improved communication is the plus side of the controversial gatekeeping role for primary care physicians in some HMOs. An additional advantage of using primary care doctors is that they are likely to do fewer tests than specialists and be less likely to call for aggressive procedures. As evidence mounts that specialists in FFS tend toward overutilization, a change in practice mode that lessens their use may be preferable.

An important part of achieving this change is the data collecting that a substantial entity can do but an individual practitioner can not. Combining cost of treatments and favorable outcomes (in terms of lower numbers of specific health problems), the plan can measure what works. Having such data in hand, it can adjust its internal "public health" program mix to achieve maximally cost-effective results. For the subscribers (and employers paying for coverage), this approach can translate into a lower rate of premium increases, as well as better health. In Chapter 3, I noted the increasing role of quality research: toting up successful outcome rates of varying procedures, determining processes that correlate best with good outcomes, and developing protocols to guide procedure decisions. "Outcomes research" and "evidence-based medicine" are the rubrics for what is now developing, and they depend on medical epidemiology. The data-gathering net encompasses clinical research by academic health centers, specialty societies, and studies sponsored by the Agency for Health Care Policy and Research. It will be enhanced by internal health plan studies applying guidelines "in the field." Not many health plans are as yet sufficiently well integrated (or have the capital needed to develop and run sophisticated information systems) to optimize this potential advantage, but it is clearly going to be a crucial element in the best health plans of the future.

In similar vein, managed care encourages or requires a style of practice that equates good care with cost-effective care, which leads to lower cost care in many cases. The Hershey Foods Corporation claims that investing a million dollars in a very strong quality monitoring program in its internal health plan saved it 7 to 10 million dollars in the first three years. [11]

One feature of HMOs that may be seen as a negative at first glance but can be a true positive is the fact that the subscriber chooses a primary care physician from among a panel screened by the HMO's management. If that screening comes to mean evaluating for quality, as found in the doctor's or hospital's record, and not just for lowest price (as has often been the case up to now), the patient will have a better basis for choice than flipping through the yellow pages or asking a friend or neighbor if she "likes" her physician. If one wants to change doctors in a managed care plan, one can more easily ascertain the credentials and experience of the choices than one can in the FFS market.

Well-integrated plans are most likely to make effective use of physician assistants, nurse practitioners, and other non-M.D. professionals. This use of nonphysician professionals will often mean improved communication with the patient at a lower cost.

In traditional medicine, Americans never had public report cards rating individual physicians and hospitals. A few years ago, Medicare released some comparative hospital mortality statistics for a few specific procedures, but abandoned this effort as criticisms mounted that the figures did not make adequate allowance for the severity of cases treated. Now, however, HEDIS is being ever more widely used and accepted as a data mold, and surveys of practice patterns, outcomes, and patient satisfaction are being published as report cards on medical groups, hospitals, and whole health plans. It is thanks to concerns about managed care, as well as to competitive incentives, that Americans now have more (if still far from adequate) information to use in making health care choices.

Finally, large, well-integrated HMOs make possible more effective use of health dollars overall. With a known budget ceiling derived from subscriber premiums, the managed care organization is compelled to balance use of its resources among its total patient population. When tests have established a patient's diagnosis with 98 percent certainty, the gatekeeper is far less likely than an FFS practitioner to order one more test "just to make certain." He will have to think about the relative need of today's patient versus that of tomorrow's, for the money pool is finite and must serve both patients. Under FFS, spending more on Patient A bears no necessary connection to spending on Patient B, which is one of the less-recognized reasons why national health costs keep rising.

This mode of practice will not, of course, be perceived as an advantage by every patient, but it does promise more cost-effective medical practice. And that should have a high priority in a country that spends far more per capita on health care than any other without noticeably better results. Ironically, what this point means is that tighter resources, when combined with global budgeting, are likely to achieve better results than the more free-spending FFS nonsystem that is inherently incapable of balancing resource use among claimant needs and services.

The Case Against Managed Care

The greatest advantages and strengths of managed care are far from being fully realized in practice. The disadvantages and weaknesses show a reverse pattern: They are more visible in present practice than they need be in principle as this new mode of health care delivery matures in organizational forms, economic incentives, and, far from least, in its culture of practice and its ethical norms.

The biggest negative is the reversed basic incentive: The health plan improves its income by spending less on its patients. In capitated care, visits, tests, and procedures are all "cost centers," and the less spent in each category, the more of the insurance premium the plan can keep. In FFS, the problem is overtreatment; in managed care it is that too little may be done. Some evidence suggests that undertreatment may happen most for the sickest and the chronically ill. HMOs are picked by employers almost entirely on price, so far. This focus on price is not only a matter of financial self-interest but also of the fact that quality measures are too crude to guide purchase decisions. Some large employers are, however, beginning to find it useful to develop report cards on plans they use and offer this information to employees to use in the annual open enrollment process.

Part of HMO financial strategy involves what is known as "cherry picking": finding ways to sign up the healthiest of potential subscribers. Cherry picking creates another problem: Those who may most need the cost advantages of managed care, because of chronic conditions or poor health, are the least likely to be reached by promotional efforts and, because income and health tend to correlate, are least likely to be able to afford traditional FFS care.

One may encounter the first managed care restriction when learning that one's employer offers only one HMO—which is the case with about half of employers who offer coverage at all. Within a closed panel HMO, restriction of choice of physicians and hospitals has probably been the most frequent and widely shared patient complaint. Your family physician may not be on the plan's list, so you have to change primary care doctors. Choice of whether to see a specialist (and which one) will often be made by the primary care physician—the gatekeeper—not the patient. Once in a plan, choice of treatment or procedure may be tightly restricted, and some denials of a particular treatment turn into lawsuits and media headlines.

Because any managed care organization will be trying to reduce use among a substantial number of subscribers, another negative for patients who have previously known only solo practitioners is the bureaucratic apparatus of clerks, account numbers, forms to sign when picking up a prescription, and so on, and so on. Indeed, even in the FFS sector, the practice of medicine has increasingly taken the form of multispecialty groups, often large enough to have their own imposing paperwork web.

For physicians, the major negatives include having to obtain clearance for certain treatments, having the plan's utilization review section press to release a patient from the hospital before the physician thinks it advisable, or being told to use the plan's official practice guideline for handling a case. Some portion of traditional professionalism (defined by the autonomy society accords its licensed practitioners) is lost to the business ethic when nonphysician managers impose organizationally approved protocols and have them rigidly administered by nurses operating from a computerized manual of approved treatments. When protocols are developed by physician teams and (within listed plan benefits) applied without nonmedical administrators being able to exert a veto, the threat to professionalism dissipates. Gripes then reflect a threat to ego.

Drug formularies present a mixed picture. A formulary is a list of approved prescription medications, and many battles are fought (by both patients and their doctors) over the relative efficacy of two drugs for curing a specific condition. Sometimes there is a substantial cost difference to the health plan without what the plan's pharmaceutical committee considers to be much difference in therapeutic value. That judgment, however, is partly financial, a cost-benefit choice on which the senior plan management may impose criteria more weighted to the money-saving side than would the formulary committee if it had free reign. (By 1998 drug costs rising at a 14 percent annual rate had become HMOs' most worrisome expense.) If the attending physician disagrees, based on his clinical experience, being second-guessed by a committee-approved list does not sit easily. Then another organizational rule is said to have come into play in some managed care plans: The doctor's contract may specify that he is not to tell the patient when he disagrees with the treatment approach required by the organization.

Doctors trying to maintain personal target incomes while receiving discounted fees and being told by plan management to limit their time per patient visit make both themselves and their patients unhappy by rushing through appointments. And patients are restive at lack of direct access to specialists—enough so that many plans have been easing that restriction, especially for patients with chronic conditions (such as asthma, diabetes, cancer, a skin condition) obviously requiring frequent specialist visits.

Some plan structures raise other problems. A major one threatens when a primary care gatekeeper works in a system where part of the income of each member of the medical group depends on holding down use of resources by all the group's doctors. Such incentive may be in the form of a "withhold" of part of the agreed income until total resource use has been determined for the year, or it may be a bonus when the total expenditure is less than anticipated. Either the stick or the carrot creates a strong incentive to be parsimonious in the use of specialists. If physician compensation takes the form of capitation plus bonus for limiting costs, primary care gatekeepers, it has been suggested, may be turned into "gate shutters."

Inconsistencies of public opinion about managed care may have their explanation in the difference between satisfaction with the care but great concern about costs, actual and prospective, as reported in the press almost daily. Another explanation may be a function of the two different sources the respondents are drawing on. One is personal experience with doctors and hospitals, which have generally been favorable; the other is the media attention given to individual anecdotes and horror stories of treatments denied or bungled. Such anecdotes appear in the press concerning actions of fee-for-service doctors' mistakes, too, but the stories do not often make explicit that the erring doctor "was a solo, fee-for-service practitioner"—which would be the appropriate equivalent to mentioning the name of the health plan whose doctor is being reported on.

The media thrust of 1996–1997 is illustrated by a study that toted up the tone of newspaper, magazine, and television news stories. Analysis of 589 citations found 5 unfavorable for every 1 favorable. Although "doctor does right by patient" will not make many headlines, there are better reasons for the extensive backlash.

Least in health importance is the bureaucratic hassle—waiting in crowded offices and delays in obtaining nonemergency specialist appointments. Such hassles are in part a consequence of organizing medical care in larger units, but they are accentuated by employers' (the purchasers, after all) resistance to premium inflation at twice or more the general rate of inflation. When auto makers realized they were spending more on health care than on steel, something was bound to give. And what gave was the luxury of having one's employer pay anything it took to enable the employee to make same-day appointments and choose specialists at will, without checking for a referral. If someone would pay for such "Cadillac" care, the HMOs would presumably be glad to provide it. But individuals don't want to, nor do their employers. Utilization review and capitated provision of care are more apparent modes of rationing than the traditional one, individual fees that not everyone could afford. The movement of health care organization from solo practitioners to large organizations with big signs on building complexes and full page ads in the papers created much better public (and legislative) targets, around which complainants could coalesce.

There are more important, though arguable, reasons behind the backlash. "Drive through" births and outpatient mastectomies are cases in point. As noted in Chapter 3, early discharge of a new mother with follow-up visits by a nurse may produce even better outcomes than staying an extra day or two in the hospital. Yet there was a real basis for complaint if the plan's nonphysician management decreed that a mother's physician could not exercise clinical judgment related to the particulars of a case to keep the mother and baby a day longer.

Mastectomies were a similar case. Some lumpectomies (a much simpler and less traumatic procedure) were confused with radical mastectomies, which of course called for more recuperation. Conversely, some plans apparently decreed that a mastectomy should be done on an outpatient basis.

State legislators responded quickly to the publicity about such situations, and the AAHP, the trade association of managed care plans, issued a policy stating that such length of stay decisions should be made by the doctor and the patient, not by plan administrators.

Too many managed care plans (not all, but it does not take many bad apples to make everyone leery of dipping into the barrel) have been tight-lipped about treatments excluded by the terms of their contracts and about the terms of their financial arrangements with physicians. Gag rules limiting what a physician might say to a patient may have been rare, but that *some* clearly did exist was enough to poison the well of public trust. Appeals processes (especially the question of independent appeals mechanisms) and criteria for covering ER expenses are also matters on which managed care plans have been deficient. Rather obviously, they have been giving priority to their own financial interests over legitimate concerns of subscriber-patients for both information and appropriate treatment. Regarding emergency room visits, even as I write these lines the industry is trying to stick to a restrictive formulation that would deny coverage unless the patient's "presenting symptoms" were adjudged to constitute an emergency as defined by a professional, rather than endorsing a "prudent layman" standard.

Strongly indicating a continuing failure of health plans to take more seriously their need to develop a context of public trust is their continuing battle against accepting responsibility for mistakes made by their doctors. When a health plan sets mandatory treatment guidelines for its doctors to follow to control the cost of care, should it not share responsibility for the quality of the care provided when the physician follows those guidelines?

The AAHP has recently beat its breast with pride over a statement of principles issued under the public relations-generated label, "Putting Patients First." (These principles include that physicians together with their patients should decide on outpatient or inpatient care after mastectomy and that plans are not to proscribe physician conversation with patients about appropriate treatments, whether or not those are all covered by the plan.)[12] One can believe they are really "putting patients first" when the AAHP develops an accreditation system that enforces its principles as a condition of membership and association approval.

What this analysis shows is that managed care can, like FFS care, be good sometimes and poor at other times at the level of doctor-patient interaction. What is clearly not good is the industry's failure to acknowledge that it is organizing the delivery of a professional service in corporate form—not just bringing the sale of tongue depressors into the twenty-first century.

The 1995–1998 backlash will die down (perhaps has done so by the time you read this book) for two reasons. One is generic to media operations and our short spans as an "attentive public" of readers, listeners, and viewers. HMO backlash has been a kind of medical war story du jour, stimulated in good part by the short time in which many millions of Americans have had to adjust to this new world of medicine. The other is that HMOs cannot afford as business competitors to restrict the care they provide in ways that subject them to ridicule in the media, whether the care is medically justified or not. Indeed, pulling back from gag orders and 24-hour birthing requirements seems to have occurred so rapidly that many state laws to forbid such practices came after the plans had already announced changes.

The clearest cost-saving element in managed care, especially of the HMO variety, has been to reduce radically the use of hospitalization. Nowhere is the impact clearer than in southern California. With intense HMO competition, the hospitalization rate was falling below 180 admissions per 1,000 enrollees, compared with a national average of 295 by 1995.[13] Kaiser announced plans to move from 232 days in 1994 to 164 in 1997 and pointed out that some California HMOs claimed use as low as 130 days per 1,000 members. (We should note that these are figures for insured patients, mostly under age 65. For the entire population, sampling projections of discharges from short-stay hospitals also show a drop, but with lower numbers: from 168 in 1980 to 117 per 1,000 in 1995.[14])

With average hospital costs in 1995 running $931 per day and $6,230 per average stay, reduced usage clearly has a beneficial impact on costs. But savings from the shift to outpatient usage (890 outpatient visits per 1,000 population in 1980; 1,471 in 1994) are one-time for each group of enrollees moved from FFS to managed care. What happens once the outpatient revolution, so to speak, has been accomplished? Will managed care costs then rise at the same rate as FFS costs in all other respects? Economies of scale in buying supplies and assembling chains of providers do not seem great enough to keep the revolution going. Moreover, technological change, which more often adds to than subtracts from systemwide expense, continues unabated. So will managed care be a lasting systemic change, or will it prove to have been nothing but a short-lived corrective to some of the excesses of fee-for-service incentives?

The Bottom Line? A Mixed Verdict

There are two basic points to make about the competition among different forms of managed care. First, all managed care plans are not born equal: Some forms are more, some less well designed to provide high-quality care. PPOs are least likely to maximize the potential advantages of the new health care delivery systems; loose HMOs with generous point-of-service options are in the middle, and closed-end HMOs of a staff/group type are best positioned for high quality at lower cost.

Second, large staff/group HMOs may enable the United States to bridge some of the long-standing gap (one hidden beneath the surface in the FFS environment) in its pattern of health care delivery between caring for individual patients and caring for populations of patients, because in the global budget world of an HMO everything done for one patient or category of patients has implications for others. Unfortunately, current competitive pressures work against the best type of HMO becoming the dominant form—at least until quality measures are so well developed and accepted that report cards mean more than being the lowest bidder.

This summary leads us to the most fundamental point about HMOs: At their potential best, they can provide a context, and therefore an incentive, for blending cost-effectiveness and quality. Done effectively, that combination would make managed care one of the great social inventions of our age.

8

Controlling Costs

Mission Impossible?

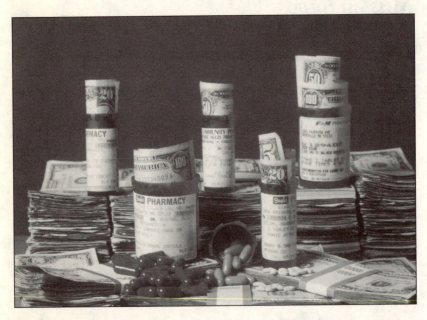

Still life—the high cost of health care. Photo courtesy of the Image Works, © M. Siluk, reprinted with permission.

HEALTH CARE PAYERS, NOT PROVIDERS or patients, are in the financial driver's seat these days. Their demands for cost containment have been heard loud and clear by competing health plans, and a real slow down in the rate of premium increases occurred between 1994 and 1996. In 1997 the rate once again exceeded inflation, and by 1998 the pace was picking up further. The Department of Health and Human Services estimates that health spending will double to $2.1 trillion a year by 2007.[1] Yet payer pressures remain intense. More than two-thirds of the under-65 population have moved from FFS coverage to managed care plans, which has been a major factor in cost reduction.

Once nearly all Americans have switched (or been switched by employers or Medicaid directors) into HMOs and PPOs, will the savings continue? Or will they prove to have been one-time reductions attributable largely to reduced hospitalization rates?

Technological changes—new medicines, new procedures, new capabilities for treating what could not be treated before—are said to account for half of the increasing cost of medicine.[2] Although many new techniques have made certain procedures spectacularly less invasive and difficult (e.g., hip replacements, cataracts, gallbladder removal, and hernia repair), they may actually increase total costs because a much greater number of patients become candidates for the procedures as their complexity and danger decrease. Also, health plans must keep abreast of the latest advances in order to be competitive, even if some are really fads, and neither they nor employer-payers have enough leverage to reduce the pace of change. In fact, a serious move was underway in Congress in 1988 to double NIH's budget within five years to $27 billion a year. So, although a 15 percent annual increase in the health research budget may be welcomed for the treatment advances one hopes will ensue, it would also have the side effect of increasing the intensity of care and thus the cost. For this and other reasons it may not be easy to keep the good news flowing once all the migration to managed care has been accomplished. So the struggle to reduce annual U.S. health care costs will continue. In this chapter I focus on what strategies might be adopted toward keeping cost increases in check, with perhaps a reasonable goal being to have health care costs rise at approximately the rate of

GDP growth (or average wage growth, which would sometimes be a tougher target).

Cost Cutting—Business Style

Costs can be attacked from two sides. The more obvious one, which dominates public perceptions, health economists' "solutions," and health plan actions, starts from the financial side. It asks ordinary business questions: How can we operate more efficiently, How can we save money by changing suppliers or buying in bulk, and so on? Or, on a larger scale, Should we merge with another firm to achieve economies of scale? With more direct connection specifically to medicine, the financially derived cost-reduction strategy asks such questions as, How can we reduce the volume and intensity of care in ways that will save money while not jeopardizing patients? Can our definitions of benefits and exclusions be used to limit our financial exposure? How far can we reduce staffing ratios of nurses to patients? And—the one that became a cause celebre in 1996–1997—Can we impose a rule that sends mothers and newborns home from the hospital in 24 hours, in normal delivery cases?

Even these latter questions flow from a financial rather than a clinical perspective. Similarly derived are precertification requirements for elective hospitalization cases, utilization review, second opinion requirements, and many gatekeeping arrangements. These procedures are not necessarily unreasonable things to do, but they did not arise primarily as responses to the question, How can we improve the quality of medical care?

The strongest approach from the financial side is, of course, the move to capitation as the dominant way of paying providers. Discounted fees in PPOs were the first direct approach to controlling what was paid to providers, but they proved to be an inadequate control and left plans unable to predict their expenses. In HMOs, fixed plan income (the number of subscribers times the monthly premium) is a recipe for Maalox moments among health plan executives if expenses cannot be closely predicted. With predictable premium income and predictable payout to providers in the form of capitation compensation, health plans have an optimal kind of global budget situation. Within that, if they can keep plan members healthy and have not made too low a bid for employers' business on behalf of members, the plans will themselves be financially healthy.

Done on a national scale, global budgeting is the primary way in which other nations keep their health care expenses far below those in the United

States. But, as we saw in Chapter 6, a national global budget requires either public financing at a specified rate or national legislation specifically limiting the payroll contributions that can be made in the private sector (such as in Germany). The day when the United States might accept such a governmentally established limit on total health spending is not yet visible on the political horizon—yet stranger things have happened when least expected.

So let's see what weapons can be employed if cost-containment is attacked from the other side. In other words, what changes designed to improve medical care can also reduce the rate of cost increase?

Better Treatments Lead to Lower Costs

Inappropriate care raises health care costs needlessly. This is true whatever the degree of inappropriateness: care that does harm; care that does no harm but is ineffective; care that is effective but costs more than an alternative, equally beneficial treatment; or care that is simply unnecessary.

Medicine is based on science, but it is called the *art* of medicine for good reason. So the question is often not simply, Is treatment A effective? We also ask, Is treatment A more effective than treatment B, and under what circumstances?

American medical culture eagerly anticipates new technologies and tends to disperse their usage widely and quickly—often before extensive trials have determined the particular circumstances and conditions for which they are most beneficial or whether they represent a definite advance over existing, less expensive approaches. Medicines and certain medical devices have to undergo a rigorous process to ensure both safety and effectiveness before they can be approved for sale by the U.S. Food and Drug Administration. But once a drug has been approved for a particular usage, additional applications develop when physicians think another usage will benefit their patients. Many of these never undergo formal testing. The fen-phen diet treatment was one such instance, and the FDA had to call a halt when the dangers of this off-label combination of two drugs approved separately gained notoriety. For surgical procedures and many treatment patterns there is no FDA-equivalent preusage review.

Can't we assume that whatever treatment most doctors prescribe for a particular condition is the right one? No—for two reasons.

The first is medical uncertainty, and it goes beyond the problem of applying science to the particular patient. Much of modern medicine lacks any substantial scientific basis. It has been estimated that perhaps only 20 percent of medical procedures in regular use have been rigorously tested in clinical trials. Consequently, just when to use which treatment is often far from being a routine decision. For instance:

- A RAND Corporation study estimated a few years ago that up to one-third of hysterectomies and angioplasties (clearing blocked arteries) were unnecessary.
- The Cesarean birth procedure has been evaluated as being substantially overused—and costing substantially more for both hospital and physician services than normal deliveries.

A surprising recent illustration of the scientific uncertainty underlying a routinely accepted diagnostic procedure is the absence of clear evidence that breast self-examination accomplishes anything beyond causing panic in many women as they do the exam each month in accord with the recommendation of the American Cancer Society. Studies around the world have failed to confirm that self-examination saves lives by early detection, and the United States Preventative Services Task Force takes a neutral position, stating that there "is insufficient evidence to recommend for or against the teaching of breast self-examination."[3]

In the absence of convincing scientific evidence for much of medical treatment, perhaps an implicit consensus exists among practicing physicians about which way to treat most conditions. Such consensus exists for some procedures, but there is no consensus regarding many treatment choices. And that leads to a second reason why one cannot assume that what a doctor does is appropriate and necessary: Treatment practices vary in different geographic locations far more than can be explained by differences in age, sex, severity of illness, or other population variables among the patients.

Dr. John E. Wennberg of Dartmouth Medical School pioneered an area of epidemiological research known as geographic practice variations in the 1980s and showed how these affected costs of care. One of his first studies found that in two Maine communities with closely similar demographics, 20 percent of women in one area's hospital had undergone a hysterectomy, but in the other town's hospital the rate was 70 percent. The cost implication? Wennberg calculated that $10 million would have been saved if both communities had had the lower rate.[4] The following are further examples of geographic variation in treatments:

- In the *Dartmouth Atlas of Health Care in the United States,* one learns that if you were a senior with a back problem in Bend, Oregon, you would be more than twice as likely to undergo surgery as the U.S. average among Medicare enrollees.[5] Back pain is a field in which there is broad uncertainty about the appropriate mode of treatment.

- San Francisco has a Medicare enrollee coronary bypass rate of 45, whereas in Sacramento, California, the rate is 62.[6] (Is being close to the state legislature, located in Sacramento, dangerous to one's health?)
- Hospitalization for asthma is three times more common in Boston than in New Haven, without any indication that Bostonians are less healthy.[7]

How can such wide variations be explained? From a finding that medicine as practiced by qualified academic medical leaders in New Haven and Boston was different enough to create a two-to-one variation in hospitalization, Wennberg inferred a significant diversity of professional opinion on the value and need of certain treatments. In instances of very slight variation across locales in the use of an operation, Wennberg found that there was professional consensus on the value of that procedure.[8]

In the absence of a scientifically validated protocol, a "practice style factor" reflecting subjective attitudes toward various treatment modalities is thought to create the now widely recognized variations. In the same vein, another prominent researcher of medical practices, Dr. David W. Eddy, wrote 15 years ago of the "tendency to follow the pack . . . to follow what is considered standard and accepted in the community," which he identified as the most basic reason for regional variations.[9]

(A rather different reason for more use of a procedure in one place than another when clear consensus on conditions for its appropriate use are absent is the phenomenon referred to as Roemer's Law: Patients are hospitalized to fill the beds available. This proposition held when hospitalization was encouraged by insurance policies and hospitals did not face DRGs and HMO-decreed limits on stays. A current equivalent may be found in the strong correlation between the number of cardiac catheterization laboratories in an area and the rate of cardiac procedures.)

By the late 1980s, the evidence of vast practice variations had become too strong to ignore—and it was likely to be an increasing problem as clinical information exploded but a physician's time to read the journals did not. What to do about it? One answer has been to develop practice guidelines and protocols: identify and codify the most successful treatment patterns.

Much of the lead in developing guidelines has been taken by the Agency for Health Care Policy and Research (AHCPR), a unit of the Public Health Service.

It focuses outcomes and effectiveness research on conditions that have a high incidence, involve high costs, or involve controversy about the effectiveness of available clinical strategies. For some physicians, the guidelines "movement" sounded too much like a "cookbook" approach to medicine, and it has been acknowledged that some early guidelines were not readily adaptable to real-world practice. Now the AHCPR operates more as an evidence-gathering entity than a producer of guidelines, and a healthy competition among medical societies and groups has sprung up to see whose guidelines will be accepted as the standard of care. Dr. Scott R. Weingarten of Cedars-Sinai Medical Center in Los Angeles sees guidelines as a way for physicians to take back control of patient care. He says that "they augment clinical decisionmaking with scientific evidence but are never a replacement for clinical expertise."[10] With this view on the rise, evidence-based guidelines are now being more widely accepted. Many health researchers see them as an important element in saving money (by not wasting money on ineffective treatments) while improving quality.

Developing guidelines requires pulling together huge data sets on whatever condition or procedure one is considering. Doing that kind of computerized analysis has become its own esoteric field, known as "medical informatics," a handy phrase for referring to "theoretical and practical aspects of information management and communication in medicine and health care."[11] There are thousands of medical treatments and procedures, so the task of devising guidelines might seem daunting and endless. There is, however, a saving element: Among the thousands of diseases and other health problems, a small number of them account for a surprisingly high proportion of all treatment needs:

- Twenty-three operations have been estimated to account for 60 percent of surgical admissions to hospitals.[12]
- Seventy percent of medical admissions in one substantial survey were occasioned by just 40 illnesses.

You might think that a program begun under President George Bush and with a mission of making health care more effective would be immune to political attack. Not so. In September 1995 AHCPR had to stand off a congressional attack stimulated by some specialists. These specialists were angered by a set of the agency's guidelines suggesting that most back pain surgery was unnecessary. A year earlier, guidelines for cataract treatment had brought flack from ophthalmologists. The guidelines program was also attacked in the House by a member who wanted to eliminate it because the government should not be telling doctors how to conduct their business. This criticism doubtless resonated strongly with those physicians who feared that guidelines would be hard and fast rules rather than useful professional information. As the agency director pointed out, in producing information that helps consumers get the best care at the least cost, AHCPR was "bound to create economic winners and losers."[13] In U.S. society economic losers try to use politics to gain what they cannot win in straightforward competition.

This point brings us to the nub of the matter. Strengthening the scientific basis of medical treatments and encouraging widespread adoption of best practices will mean not only better medical care but also more medical bang for the buck. To illustrate the problem, consider advances in imaging (CAT scans, MRIs, PET scans—all the new tools for taking pictures of our insides), which are immeasurably beneficial for some purposes but which can also be used wastefully. For example, common lower back and other muscular pains, when not severe but bothersome enough to warrant an office visit, may be treated with analgesics and exercises. Or one could do an MRI to see what the trouble is. Which is appropriate depends on what the doctor learns when taking the patient's history. If the pain is felt by a patient in otherwise excellent health, who exercises regularly, but who has just done three days of lifting and unpacking boxes after a home move, the conservative (i.e., less complicated, less intrusive, less high-tech) treatment is probably in order. If the doctor instead calls for the MRI, that's a probably unnecessary and certainly more expensive first response. The test would in this instance presumably confirm the physician's judgment that only a simple treatment was needed, which means that the test was effective for diagnosis—but not *cost* effective.

Physicians have, of course, always been concerned about effectiveness. But that's no longer enough. The first part of the term cost effective opens up a whole new world of concern. Not only do we ask which of two or three medicines, treatments, procedures is the most effective, we now also need to ask, Which of two treatments deemed effective costs the least? And if one is only marginally more effective than another (e.g., improving a diagnosis from 98 percent certainty to 99 percent, or making a moderate muscular ache disappear in 12 hours instead of 36), is it worth the extra cost? If the difference is only 10 cents, little is lost by taking the more expensive route. But what if the difference is $100 versus $1,000 (and some medicines do have order of magnitude differences in price yet only marginal differences in effectiveness for a certain class of cases)? Then it matters.

Another kind of money-saving efficiency, one increasingly being incorporated into group practices and the resource plans of managed care organizations, is the use of professional personnel less highly trained and compensated than M.D.s: physician assistants, nurse practitioners, and trained nurse midwives. A family-oriented maternity center in Philadelphia staffed mostly by nurse midwives not only costs less than a comparable facility staffed entirely with physicians, it also had a Cesarean birthrate 2.5 times lower than in the teaching hospital with which it was affiliated. Cost-effectiveness concepts can also be applied by regionalization of the most expensive equipment and the most costly and complicated surgical procedures. Use of hospice concepts (providing palliative care and human warmth in a nonhospital setting for patients judged to be within six months of dying) saves money while improving life's last experience.

Asking physicians to incorporate the cost element into their judgments constitutes a near-revolution in the practice of medicine. It is not easily accommodated or happily accepted, yet will probably be one of the most decisive elements in trying to reach a societally acceptable rate of health care cost growth for the United States. A medical strategy of cost containment has great promise. Instead of starting by cutting costs and hoping to avoid inadequate care in the process, the medical approach directs its efforts at ensuring that treatments are safe, effective, and appropriate to a particular patient's condition. The by-products of improving certainty about what works are avoiding unnecessary health care expenses and targeting resources toward what does work.

Two kinds of research have come to the forefront in recent years as the need for cost effectiveness was manifested by studies showing overuse and the too-quick spread of many technologies and treatments. "Outcomes research" is the label of one; "evidence-based medicine" is the tag given to the other by its proponents.

Accreditation review for hospitals used to cover structure (facilities, staffing levels, equipment) and processes (protocols the hospital employed in treating patients for a variety of medical conditions). Medical outcomes (Did the patient recover from whatever necessitated the treatment? Did he regain full ability to engage in normal daily activities? Did he have any lasting unwanted side effects?) were not much examined until just a few years ago. One good reason was that the records did not contain the information needed for such an evaluation.

In the late 1980s Dr. Paul M. Ellwood (who coined the term health maintenance organization) pushed for the creation of what he called an "outcomes management" system—a national database covering clinical, financial, and health outcomes of treatments. Clinicians would draw on this information

bank as they made treatment choices. Although no single national data reposi-
tory of this nature yet existed in the late 1990s, components were being developed in a variety of organizations and settings. The HEDIS system, now officially required by Medicare, among other payers, is national though not all
inclusive. NCQA published HEDIS data on 330 health plans in late 1997. And
the nation's largest HMO, Kaiser Permanente, has committed hundreds of millions of dollars to developing computerized data systems that include outcomes of treating its millions of patients. It plans to use this information to de-
vise cost-effective protocols for its physicians. AHCPR's guidelines-oriented
research program now emphasizes establishing links between competing clinical strategies and their outcomes. The new focus on outcomes data will supplement rather than replace examination of processes, for outcomes knowledge is
of the fullest value when combined with knowledge of the processes used in
treatment. Unless we know what processes were used we won't know what to
change to improve the outcomes rate at a particular hospital. As guidelines are
devised and technology assessments are made, tracking the outcomes from the
use of protocols serves to improve the protocols. By gathering financial along
with medical outcomes information, relative cost effectiveness of alternative
treatments can be determined.

A recent technology assessment based on an outcomes study provides a
good example of the combined treatment and financial importance of such research. It concerns the use of home fetal monitors, intended to prevent women
at high risk of premature labor from giving birth too early. Strapped around
the abdomen, and used at a daily cost of $30 to $100, this warning signal device has had conflicting results in small studies. A Kaiser facility in Santa Clara,
California, followed over 2,400 high-risk pregnancies. All of the women were
intensively educated about the symptoms of early labor before being assigned
to one of three groups for comparing daily monitoring with daily and weekly
phone contact with nurses. The finding was that weekly calls were as effective
in preventing preterm births as the daily machine monitoring, at very much
lower cost. And elimination of the monitoring would produce an additional
savings because drugs to stop contractions were mostly used with the women
on daily monitoring. Stopping both maximized savings without increasing
prematurity.[14]

Another very simple clinical trial recently measured the effectiveness of using warming blankets during a patient's surgery. Because operating rooms are
kept quite cool, patients' body temperatures drop a few degrees, causing mild
hypothermia. In someone at risk for a heart attack, that's dangerous. In a 1997
test, 150 patients were covered with special warming blankets, whereas another

150 were covered with the standard paper sheets. The outcome: Those in the first group were 55 percent less likely to suffer heart complications. Change in practice: The warming blanket is rapidly becoming a standard protocol for major operations. It adds to costs a little but saves much more, in both lives and money.[15]

Evidence-based medicine can be described as using research information prospectively. It means that a doctor contemplating what treatment to use goes beyond his own training and clinical experience to look up the most recent medical journal literature relating to the condition the patient presents. Combining what he finds in searching the medical research literature with his clinical experience, particularities of his patient, and pathophysiological knowledge, the physician can then proceed with the most scientifically valid approach available. Proponents of this approach want more than doing literature searches before acting; they want physicians to learn enough about methodology to be able to apply formal rules of evidence for evaluating the quality of the research they read. This approach, they argue, is both enabled and necessitated by the spread of randomized clinical trials in the past 30 years.

The new paradigm challenges the physician to pay less attention to expert opinion, much of it not undergirded by scientific analysis, and to perform independent assessment of the most recent clinical trial evidence. It requires easy access to expensive computerized data bases (at the bedside, or at least at the nurses' station and in each doctor's office) and the training of a new generation of physicians.

Because there are so many areas in which outcomes and process findings have not yet been able to establish validated guidelines—and because biomedical knowledge increases extremely rapidly—the evidence-based approach may be a significant corollary to outcomes research and guidelines. For instance, if a doctor usually has few pneumonia cases, she may not have read a 1997 report on a study of 14,000 over-65 patients hospitalized with pneumonia. But a search of recent literature (made much easier than before by use of the database Medline on the Internet) would alert her that antibiotic administration within 8 hours of hospital arrival and blood culture collection within 24 hours correlated strongly with lowering 30-day mortality. (These process-of-care measures were used in only half the pneumonia cases in some states, which demonstrates a real value to doing evidence-based searches.)

These new approaches relate to cost effectiveness, which we noted earlier is not easily grafted onto a doctor's historic concern for effectiveness in itself. During the halcyon period of widespread fee-for-service health insurance (especially for hospitalization), when treatments generally cost little and frequently did little as well, physicians could often ignore cost considerations. Relatively open-ended health care finance permitted patients and doctors to agree that everything should be done that would have even very slight benefit. In the managed care context, a health plan budget fixed for the short run by its preset funding per patient makes it imperative that providers learn to think in terms of balancing the needs of the whole population covered, so that some are not left without important care because others drained the money pool for treatments of negligible or dubious benefit.

This is the tenor of the argument for strong use of cost-effectiveness analysis as most forcefully articulated in a series of articles in the *Journal of the American Medical Association* (*JAMA*) in the mid-1990s by Dr. David M. Eddy. He starts with the premise that health care costs cannot be allowed to keep on taking a larger share of GDP each year—from 5 percent in 1960 to 13.6 in 1996. The greater its share, the less is available for everything from education and housing to higher cash wages or landing astronauts on Mars. Instead, health care cost inflation should simply keep pace with GDP. To achieve this goal, he argues two controversial propositions, one with positive, one with negative consequences:

1. We must ration health services, which he defines as "not covering from public or shared resources some treatments that are acknowledged to have benefit."[16]
2. Carefully done cost reductions can actually serve to raise the quality of care overall.

At this point you may ask, Why not just cut out inefficiencies and administrative waste instead of doing anything as distasteful as rationing care? Because administrative costs are not the only ones that keep increasing. After accounting for general and specifically medical price inflation, population increase, and aging, one-third of cost increases each year flow from greater volume and intensity of health services. New technologies, new medicines, and new procedures are the stuff of which new medical miracles are built. They also mean new expenses. So there's a strong argument for making the most of what we apply to health care.

The easiest use of cost effectiveness comes in cases where two medications are equally effective but one costs twice as much as the other. Put the less expensive one in the health plan's drug formulary. That's simple (unless a physician finds that one of her patients is an exception and only responds to the more expensive ones, in which case plans must be flexible).

Now let's look at breast cancer screening for one of Dr. Eddy's examples of true rationing.[17] Randomized trials show that biennial screening for women 50 to 70 years of age reduces 10-year mortality by a third. For patients below age 50, studies about the effectiveness of screening have varied results and no benefit has been proven. For ages 70 to 74, the reduction in mortality may be 8 percent, and over 75 there is no evidence of value. Using data from a real plan, he found that 22 percent of women aged 30 to 40 were screened annually; 60 percent in ages 40 to 50; 69 percent in ages 50 to 75, and 57 percent in ages 75 to 85. Using estimates from clinical trial findings, about 909 women's lives will be saved over 15 years with those rates of screening.

But hypothesize a new strategy in which mammography would be discouraged below age 50 and above 75 but expanded to reach 95 percent of those between 50 and 75. The 15-year number of deaths prevented would increase by 297, while costs would be reduced by $150 million. That's a win-win: higher systemic quality *and* lower costs. Eddy believes physician analysts can find many similar opportunities to enhance care while reducing costs by reducing low-value treatments and switching some of the funds saved to broadening high-value practices.

Dr. Eddy acknowledges a problem. When a low-value treatment is not given, the patient and physician who perceived a possible benefit, real or not, will see a decline in quality. (The patient could still pay for the denied treatment outside of his health plan, of course, but that is not likely be considered a satisfactory response.) There is a paradox here: Transfers of resources like those in the breast cancer example do add benefits while reducing costs; yet in the process some people lose a benefit and are harmed. How can one claim a net increase in quality from the rationing process?

The answer lies in how we measure an increase in quality for a health plan, and here it is best to quote Dr. Eddy:

> First, health plans are responsible for the health of a population. All the members paid into the resource pool that is being drawn on to provide care, and they all deserve to be counted in any measure of benefit or quality. Second, health plans are given finite resources for doing this: the dues, premiums, and payments provided by the members, businesses, and governments. . . . The objective is to maximize the health of the population it serves, subject to the limits on its resources, and the proper measure of quality is how well it does that.[18]

This definition can be called making the best of a zero-sum game: When the money pool is fixed, whatever is spent on one subgroup is no longer available for spending on another. It cannot be resolved by doing both unless participants are willing to keep adding to the common pool. It is clear that employers and governments are no longer willing to do that. As they become intent on reducing their rate of cost increase to release resources for other purposes, they either cut down directly on the services they are willing to finance, or they shift more of the costs to the patient pool. But by mid-1997 the share of employer-sponsored health care paid by employees had risen to a point at which more and more employees were turning down the offered coverage and taking their chances—"going bare" as it is called in the insurance industry.[19] And if many of those turning down coverage are young and healthy, then the per employee costs for the covered group will rise because the plan will have a higher proportion of older workers needing more services.

These relationships exemplify a basic dilemma for both health insurance plans and the nation. Either Americans restrain costs by the kinds of hard choices advocated by Dr. Eddy and others, which are increasingly being practiced by the most sophisticated health plans, or they sacrifice the opportunity to do much else that is desirable because they will have let health care siphon off a disproportionate share of total societal resources.

That the choices are hard ones—even agonizing—should not be minimized. The good physician wants to do everything she can for the patient she is treating at the moment. Asking her to consider limiting in any way treatment for patient A in the interest of having funds available also for patients B, M, Z, and so on is perceived by many physicians as a violation of their ethical code. However, the ethical injunction to do everything one can for the individual patient has always, in fact, had a silent clause: within a given financial context. Before World War II, when there was little health insurance, especially for nonhospital treatments, doctors often had to consider their patients' financial situations when deciding on a course of treatment. They would provide charity care for some, but they could not make that the basis of a practice. Therefore, they also had to choose modes and extents of treatment partly on the basis of cost. Both physicians and patients were badly spoiled in the postwar era of FFS health financing. Its open-endedness enabled all parties to largely forget that there were any limits to treatment. And the cost of treating patient A had no discernible effect on what one did for patient X. Now, with most Americans in fixed pools of money (capitation payments times the number of subscribers), there are very real funding limits. It just won't work to say that one will refuse to recognize these limits when they are not indefinitely expandable, as Americans were coddled into believing in well-insured FFS days. So the conflict between saving lives (or, less dramatically, making them maximally healthy) and staying within what is almost universally a fixed budget today is perhaps the most basic of clinical-financial dilemmas—and Americans have hardly begun to face it.

So, what do you think? What would you do? What should the nation do? If the preferred answer is to add resources so that cost effectiveness can be avoided, then the question is: How much more would each individual like to pay? Employers and governments will simply not keep the money tap at the full-open setting any longer. And with a national global budget beyond the U.S. political will so far, cost effectiveness is the best card in the deck.

Can the United States Change Its Culture of Medicine?

We have discussed economists' cost-containment ideas and ways that medical effectiveness can be enhanced by physicians. But the most fundamental reason for this nation's ranking as having the most expensive health care in the world is not a matter of modes of payment or of procedures, treatments, medications, and diagnostic tests. It is the *culture* of medical care, a culture shared by physicians and patients alike. And its theme song is "Don't just stand there; do something."

Lynn Payer, in her book *Medicine and Culture,* noted that doctors very often use the term "aggressive" to describe an appropriate approach to diagnosis and treatment. This penchant for lots of action is so strong, she reports, that when a blood pressure study group recommended easing up on drug treatment for mild hypertension in favor of diet and exercise, they urged that even these non-drug therapies be "pursued aggressively." She suggests that this medical behavior reflects the frontier effect: that anything is possible "if only the natural environment . . . could be conquered. Disease also could be conquered, but only by aggressively ferreting it out diagnostically and just as aggressively treating it."[20] The seemingly inherent tendency in the United States toward maximizing treatment is pushed even further by physician fears of malpractice law suits, which lead them to practice "defensive medicine"—defending against trial lawyers.

In contrast, Payer quotes a British doctor-writer who says that medical students there "are taught to question the need for things being done. You are trained to think what is really necessary, why do you do it, what the results are. Does modern medical technology do any good? Is it better than not doing anything?"

Because the British health delivery system operates with the very definite cost constraints of an annually appropriated national budget, the equipment and facilities available for patients' needs have been far less than in the United States. Kidney dialysis was used to delineate the difference a few years ago. In the United States, Medicare was amended in 1972 by singling out this one disease and making dialysis patients of any age eligible for Medicare. As technology improved, older and older patients went on dialysis, with little effort on the part of doctors to question its value for any one patient. In Britain, the "painful prescription" was for the physician to tell the family of an ESRD patient over 55 that Uncle Joe was "a bit crumbly" and therefore not a good candidate for dialysis.[21] This excuse is easier to say than, "Sorry, we don't have enough machines or money to include everyone who could benefit from dialysis."

Aggressive style further aggravates the cost problem in the United States when it is combined with another American trait: faith in technological gadgetry. Many medical observers have remarked in recent years that the younger doctors seem not to be trained in listening carefully to a patient's presentation and doing a good history, which would often obviate any need for laboratory tests. Testing becomes a substitute for a good doctor-patient dialogue, yet it very often costs more. The technological imperative also shows up in competition to be the first with a new or improved treatment. Laudable in itself, the urge to innovate can suck up resources that might more rationally extend a lot of lives for the cost of saving one—say a premature baby weighing just a pound whose medical treatments may run up a bill of $500,000 before getting out of the hospital. And some have been "saved" only to face a life of incapacitating disability that will burden their families during their entire lifetimes.

As I write, a news service reports that suburbanites trying futilely to fight head cold viruses by using antibiotics (which work on bacterial infections, but not on viruses) are responsible for strong mutant strains of bacteria that then require more aggressive antibiotics to fight them. A researcher who has studied antibiotic use says that physicians "feel they are pushed against a wall" by patients who, told to go home and take vitamin C instead of an antibiotic, decide they have a bad doctor. Enough doctors succumb to the pressure to have produced the irony of more affluent suburbs suffering from too much care: Overuse of antibiotics produces a higher rate of resistant strains in such areas. Simply using symptom-ameliorating products and letting nature take its course with a cold is hard for most Americans to do.

Just like doctors, U.S. patients have a culture of unrestrained medical expectations. Although 70 percent of treatments are attributable to decisions made by physicians, those on the receiving end must accept their share of what the insurance industry calls "moral hazard," meaning overuse of resources simply because insurance will pay for it. The whole U.S. attitude toward life and death probably is, I suspect, the larger factor in the nation's problem of medical profligacy. The slow acceptance of hospice in the United States, with its orientation toward a peaceful death rather than a last-ditch battle to keep one alive a few more days, is a good indicator of national attitudes. Americans tend to think of themselves as prolonging life when they use tubes and technology on a person whose life would end without "extraordinary" intervention. In most other cultures, this approach would be labeled (more accurately, in my view) prolonging death. In the United States more than in other Western nations death is the enemy, not the last part of life. That attitude means Americans, doctors and patients both, are far more likely than the French, or British, or Germans to choose an extra treatment (paid for by a third-party insurer) that may keep a cancer patient alive, technically at least, for an extra few days. And that attitude partially explains how the 6.4 percent of Medicare beneficiaries who died in 1994 accounted for 20.6 percent of all Medicare payments.

Conversely, compare Americans' vehement pursuit of whatever will return them to health after an illness with their unwillingness to pursue preventive health measures and healthier lifestyles with similar vigor. Flu shots are missed by a significant portion of the at-risk age groups, many parents still do not see that their children are immunized on schedule, and obesity is rising as Americans make up in large quantities of low-fat calories the few high-fat items they have foregone.

In the late nineteenth century and much of the twentieth, improved life expectancy in the United States was the result less of technological marvels in medicine than of improved sanitation, drinking water, and public health attacks on contagious diseases. As the century ends, we know what the equivalent nonmedication lifestyle should be: no smoking, very moderate drinking, aerobic exercise, and adherence to the revised food pyramid. Somehow, it seems easier to many to take their chances and then count on medical care to bail them out of illness. Americans have medicalized good health and thus contributed to its great expense.

There is one countermovement, but it is not exactly spreading like wildfire: the use of advance directives—living wills and durable powers of attorney for health care. In various forms these ways of telling our families and our doctors what we want—or, frequently, do not want—by way of treatments when hit by heart attacks, strokes, cancer, and similar medical events are available in most states. For example, a form used in California a few years ago provided a variety of instructions one could indicate as incorporating one's wishes, ranging from

> I do not want life-sustaining treatment . . . if the burdens of treatment outweigh the expected benefits. I expect my agent to consider the relief of suffering and the quality as well as the extent of the possible extension of my life

through

> I want life-sustaining treatment to be provided unless I am in a coma which my doctors reasonably believe to be irreversible.

to

> I want my life to be prolonged to the greatest extent possible without regard to my condition, the chances I have for recovery or the cost of the procedures.

Hospitals are now required by federal law to inquire of Medicare patients whether they have an advance directive and give them a chance to set one up (but not to require that they do so). The law is not universally adhered to, and the majority of people either are not aware of advance directives or may find the subject too distasteful as an admission of the possibility of death. Yet the development of advance directives does indicate that a new popular standard is emerging: that the quality of one's life is a legitimate factor in deciding whether temporal extension of one's life is worth great expense or great pain.

One cost-increasing expectation that means little medically but a lot in terms of patient satisfaction is that the amenities of care, especially when hospitalized, will be preserved at the highest standard. These amenities include semiprivate or private rooms, phones, and television—and probably now computer, fax, and Internet connections. It means pleasant as well as nutritious meals. It means quick attention for even minor needs. All these amenities are nice, and I would prefer not to do without them. But patients in most nations do without them, which is presumably a meaningful reason for the lower costs of health care in those nations. My guess is that losing some of the amenities of care would cause more backlash than the withdrawal of some significant medical treatments. In fact, some hospitals are raising costs these days by building special wings and suites for preferred customers.

I've described the aggressive, activist stance that has ruled the American health care roost since World War II, which is roughly when treatment became much more effective, expensive, and, fortunately, reimbursable through insurance for more and more people. But what happens to the "Do something!" syndrome in the age of managed care?

So far, it is reasonable to assume that the activist ethos underlies much of the managed care backlash that began about 1995. And it has had some effect in pushing the "Do less" syndrome back a bit: It has brought about the right to appeal denials of treatments, the drive-through limitations for birthing and mastectomies, an so on. But that's in the very short run.

In the longer run, public expectations will be forced to change. Systemwide cost increases that annually exceed the rate of inflation and of GDP growth are simply not sustainable: Americans won't let health care eat up half the national income each year. Simply from reading major medical journals and research-based reports one may hazard a guess that slow—sometimes imperceptible—change is occurring in the physician community. Less invasive procedures now compete with more invasive ones in an increasing proportion of situations. Cost effectiveness, although far from widely adopted in toto, is gaining adherents, probably mostly among younger doctors with newer training and professional experience entirely in managed care situations. Insurance patterns no longer lead the doctor toward hospitalization for patients just to make treatment eligible for reimbursement. Physicians as well as laypersons are learning to look to lifestyle and diet changes as frequently the best medicine for those at risk for some major chronic diseases. Although no figures are at hand on the number of people who have adopted living wills or other forms of advance directives—which tend to embody less aggressive expectations on the part of patients—it is probably safe to say that their use is increasing. And health plans run on a capitation basis embody a major (if often unwilling from the viewpoint of the patient) organizational change that is ineluctably going to produce a sea change in U.S. medical culture. Looking into a very murky crystal ball, I will hazard the guess that "Do something!" will increasingly have to compete with "Is this trip necessary?" as the mantra of American health care. Right now it's a battle, exemplified in an oversimplified way as fee-for-service versus managed care. In time, maybe a via media will develop on principles yet to be articulated.

9

....

A Sensible Wild Idea

Universalize Medicare

Warning: *This chapter is intentionally speculative and provocative. It may require hard thinking. Why? Because there is no easy solution, politically or economically, to the basic dilemma of health care in the United States. And because the incrementalist thinking that dominates public discussion of major issues in this age of diminished expectations, distrust of government, and unthinking glorification of economic individualism is increasingly proving itself an abysmal failure in the area of health care. So put your "little gray cells" to work; challenge my proposals for achieving a better health care system with universal coverage—but can you suggest a more realistic way to achieve universal health insurance for Americans?*

More than 20,000 people crowd the start line for the annual "Race for the Cure" to raise money for breast cancer research programs in Royal Oak, Michigan, April 25, 1998. Singer Olivia Newton-John, a breast cancer survivor, was among the participants who turned out for the event. Photo courtesy of Associated Press/Paul Warner, reprinted with permission.

P OLITICAL ECONOMIST Charles Lindblom achieved lasting professional fame half a century ago by describing American policy making as a process of "muddling through." More formally, political scientists call this type of policy making the doctrine of incrementalism: American policies change by small increments, not giant steps. This characterization is not always accurate, however.

President Franklin D. Roosevelt's New Deal was a major exception. The desperate conditions of the Great Depression made possible major policy innovations, from Social Security to the Securities Exchange Commission. The combination of the Kennedy assassination, President Lyndon B. Johnson's own extraordinary political skills, and a strong national economy and federal budget surplus enabled Johnson to declare a War on Poverty and move the nation toward what he modestly termed the Great Society. Civil rights legislation and the passage of Medicare and Medicaid are among the lasting vital elements of the mid-1960s, before the Vietnam War convulsed the country.

As the post–World War II surge in economic growth slowed after 1973, so too did the urge to initiate large federal programs. In the 1980s the public responded favorably to the ideological stance of President Ronald Reagan, who saw government as the problem, not the solution. Although President Bill Clinton was elected with only a plurality of the national vote in 1992 and proclaimed himself a new kind of centrist Democrat, he tried for major policy change in two areas.

One was welfare reform, where his emphasis on work, responsibility, and time limits for public assistance meshed well enough with the congressional Republicans' approach to achieve a substantial, if still controversial, change in how the nation's responsibilities to its least fortunate citizens would be pursued. The other area was, of course, health care, as discussed in Chapter 3. In the wake of the Clinton Health Security Plan debacle, something not much foreseen in anyone's crystal ball happened: The private sector, stimulated by a an employer-payer revolt, picked up the ball and began what we know as the managed care revolution.

Is that the end of it for this generation? I think not. The churning, unpredictable, rapidly changing mix of new organizational forms, new modes of insurer-provider relationships, and steadily increasing percentage of unin-sured adults under 65 does not constitute a stable equilibrium.

Americans Will Live with the
Dilemma—But Not Forever

The basic dilemma—Is health care a market good or a public good?—is one that Americans reject, at least in stark terms. The United States predominantly sells health services on a private market (for those under 65), and employer provision of health insurance is perceived as the organizational base of the system. Yet Americans skew the market with a variety of private and public inter-ventions to distribute this very basic good differently than would a pure mar-ket. Cost shifting (a hospital charging well-insured patients more to make up what it loses on the uninsured) and public subsidies have permeated the pic-ture.

With private and public payers both in revolt, health care is now facing the economists' ultimate truth: There is no such thing as a free lunch. Long accus-tomed to the privileged position of simply presenting its bill to society and re-ceiving in payment an ever-increasing share of GDP, the health care-industrial complex has recently been learning that both business and government see health care as but one among many competitors for a piece of the financial pie.

For now, government will continue to supplement the market by subsidiz-ing care for those who lack the money to buy care privately, as well as for se-niors of all incomes. Nonprofits and charities contribute substantially to the supply of medical services, often in clinics that are vital to the life of poverty-stricken communities. But when the nation has 42 million Americans totally uninsured for health care and the public sector share of total medical expendi-tures is very close to equaling the private sector share, it would be fatuous to expect the combination of nonprofits and bad debt write-offs from for-profit entities to fill the uninsured gap.

Let's start with the existing parameters. Privately financed health care is not something most Americans buy personally. The lion's share of it has been fi-nanced by employers since World War II. But that share is declining because employers are selecting plans that call upon employees to pay larger de-ductibles and copayments each year, making workers pay all of the premiums for their dependents, and discontinuing coverage for under-65 retirees. As noted earlier, some of the current growth in the ranks of the uninsured is at-tributed to workers turning down employer-offered coverage because they find their share unacceptably high. With the trend again upward in premiums, the workings of the market in the foreseeable future will further undermine the existing system.

Americans may well limp along for a few more years with gradual changes. As costs continue to rise but payers balk and legislators respond to unhappy constituents by mandating particularities of coverage in health plans, smaller employers may increasingly offer a single, low-cost plan that has limits on coverage as sharp as the law allows, plus high copays. Already, over half of mid-size firms offer only a single HMO plan. Many large corporations now offer cafeteria choices: differing coverages at differing prices, but with the employer paying a fixed amount no matter whether you choose a low-priced plan or a better one that requires you to make a supplementary premium payment. These employers will say, "Why undergo the annual pain and strain of choosing coverage details? We're not expert in this anyway. So let's move to a voucher system: We'll send a check for a specified number of dollars to whatever health plan the employee designates." When they do, legislatures will get into the act by trying to protect the employee consumer with rules regarding what information the health plan sales people must supply—as the government has mandated for Medigap plans for seniors.

Employers would then be tempted to let the dollar value of their contributions slip over time. When inflation then eroded the value of the vouchers so that employees could not buy a satisfactory benefit package, this system would also fail. The hemorrhaging of the percent insured might be stanched for a time, replaced by a less politically visible bulge in the number of underinsured as the vouchers failed to keep pace with inflation and bought less and less each year. The game of financial musical chairs would become even more frantic as people went to ERs for care they could not pay for but which institutions were legally or ethically bound to provide. The payers left holding the bag would then try desperately (but often unsuccessfully) to pass it along to someone else.

The employer-based system may turn out to have been just a temporary arrangement by which U.S. society moved into the age of effective, expensive medical care after World War II. What will happen when the slumbering giant of public opinion becomes persuaded that major change is worth risking, rather than further deterioration of an increasingly unsustainable patchwork? What particular mix of private and public is most likely? Most desirable?

It is easier to say what will not develop than what will. Having only a very murky crystal ball, I will limit myself to brief mention of scenarios least likely to develop and then sketch what I think would be most desirable. Whether the desirable will prove to be politically practicable is of course unknowable in the

abstract. But one of the great advantages of the untidiness of the undisci-
plined, undeferential, populistic U.S. political system is that it is always open to
major change—which sometimes actually happens.

The safest prediction is that whatever strategy Americans adopt, it will not
involve a national health service in the British sense. Only in public education
at the K–12 level has this nation adopted a government-owned and -operated
institutional form as the organizing principle for a major sector of national
life, and that institution is run at the local level. Let's look at some other possibilities.

Clinton Redux?

How a few years can change things! In 1994, Clinton's Health Security Plan was
easily (if somewhat inaccurately) tagged a radical, Big Government route to
universal health care coverage. Then came the thousand and one nicks and
bites of what we can call little private governments, that is, organizations that
make rules one has to live by. When employers awakened, seemingly overnight,
to the realization that health care was one of their most costly components of
production, they said, Enough! No more double-digit annual premium increases!

Insurers responded by offering PPOs, IPAs, and so on. HMO became probably the best-known domestic acronym since the alphabet soup of the New
Deal. The private sector substituted all kinds of micromanagement for the rejected Clinton Plan: restrictions on coverage; clearance hurdles worthy of an
Olympic contest before seeing a specialist; "quicker and sicker" discharges of
hospital patients, all too often into a subacute void of rehabilitative care; doctors told (by formulary committees on which they had representatives, but
still, told) that their preferred medication was too expensive, so please use only
Drug X.

The irony is that the president's concept would have been no more intrusive
and would have left greater choice in place. Consumer and small business
coalitions called "health alliances" would have been the purchasing organizations for a standard benefits package. People could sign up through their employers, or individually if not employed, for a plan of their choice, fee for service or HMO. Employers would pay 80 percent, employees 20 percent.
Subsidies would enable even the lowest income people and small businesses
to participate. In other words, the system would have remained largely
employment-based, with competition among health plans to get businesses to
sign up with them.

What, then, was wrong? Americans did not like the government supervision required by the plan. The alliances would be government-sponsored. Every employer would be obligated to insure its employees. A standard benefits package would be defined by the government, providing a basis for comparing prices and quality among competitors. Worst of all from the viewpoint of established economic interests, the Clinton plan would set a ceiling on insurance premium increases. One might suppose people would see that as a good thing, but a ceiling on payments for some people is a ceiling on incomes for others—and those whose incomes are at stake are politically better organized. Ironically, Clinton's plan was probably the least disturbing to the employment-based way of handling health care that could possibly accomplish the goal of achieving universal coverage. But the time for that approach has come and gone.

Look North of the Border?

The Canadian health care system has been the lodestar for many American health care reform proponents. Once one gets over the big political hurdle that it replaces the private health insurance industry with a national health insurance system, it has much to recommend it. It covers everyone. It retains federalism rather than moving all decision making to the national level. It is strongly egalitarian: Everyone carries the same insurance card and is eligible for the same care in the same facilities. Fee-for-service, and therefore free choice of physicians, is the mode of practice. Doctors don't have insurance clerks second-guessing their treatment decisions, and patients don't have to seek permission from an official gatekeeper in order to see a specialist. Because hospitals are under centralized global budgets in each province, Canada has an ability Americans might envy to rationalize distribution of equipment and major services into regional centers.

If it all seems too good to be true, there's a reason: It is. It does fulfill the criterion of universal coverage, but in some other respects, it creates obstacles to an improved mode of medical practice.

Exactly because it underwrites the lone duck mode of practice, it makes integration of care difficult. With a higher ratio of primary care doctors than in the United States, it automatically has something of an informal gatekeeper referral system, and personal physicians may keep track of Canadians' visits to specialists. But the system does not ensure a seamless health record, as a well-integrated one might. Canada has had little HMO development. Great? Maybe not, for as we saw in Chapter 7, HMOs have at least a potential for better and more cost-effective treatment than individual fee-for-service care, and Canada has not developed that potential very much. With the national government trying to reduce its health care financing commitment while still telling provinces what services they must provide, a major political storm is said to be brewing over their version of a health care entitlement.

What about the Canadian cost advantage? It is considerable, deriving from a global budgeting system. It may, however, actually be too great at this time, to judge from the insistent call for more resources if existing services are to be maintained (see Chapter 6). And some of Canada's ways of saving money would be extremely hard to sell in the United States. Some U.S. hospitals are building special pavilions for wealthy patients, and a U.S. health care consultant has even argued that everyone should have a private room, with not only a television but a video library and perhaps a networked computer. In Canada, the four-person ward is more common than the semiprivate room. And in-room television sets and telephones are not part of the coverage in some provinces.

More to the heart of the matter—and an aspect rarely mentioned by American admirers of Canadian health care—its lower cost derives in part from more limited scope of coverage than is provided in most private sector U.S. health plans. Hospitalization and medically necessary treatments are indeed universal, but the nationally mandated program does not include prescription medicines, dental care, or home health care. Prescription coverage is like Medicare in the United States: It is covered only in the hospital. Only 35 percent of drug costs are paid for publicly.[1]

Provinces have varying supplemental programs of their own devising, and Canadian employers (who many Americans proponents of the Canadian system are surprised to learn have any role at all) provide private coverage for some of what is left out. For example, the auto manufacturers provide private insurance covering semiprivate hospital rooms, improving on the ward coverage of the Ontario-provincial plan.

Desirable as some aspects of the Canadian system may be, U.S. history—general and of health care in particular—is too different to warrant copying the Canadian system as Americans' way out of the health care dilemma. However, whatever form the eventual achievement of a universal coverage system takes, two prerequisites found in Canada and in Britain, Germany, and other European nations will have to be part of the picture. One is global budgeting (already in place everywhere except the United States). The other is some limitation on the scope of coverage in line with the concept (admittedly very difficult to reduce to specifics) of "basic" services, with private, supplemental services that could be purchased personally or received as an employee benefit, as in Canada.

Set a Global Budget for Public Health Care

Given the explosive cost growth of Medicare as originally designed, the government found that it had to revise the payment system with DRGs and RBRVS to reduce the fiscal drain. But it is still an essentially open-ended system in which usage determines annual cost rather than an annual budget setting limits on usage. It should remain an entitlement (i.e., if you are of an included age, you are covered, without a means test, period), but an entitlement within an annually appropriated budget. A global budget for Medicaid was proposed just a few years ago and quickly rejected, with legislators looking over their shoulders with fear and trepidation at the AARP. When the medical advantages of a global budget as a stimulus to cost effectiveness become better known, however, it should be possible to overcome the prejudices of the past (and the screams of providers). From the viewpoint of Office of Management and Budget economists, global budgeting is a device for predictability and control of expenditures. From the viewpoint of Congress, it would be a better way to reduce the rate of Medicare expenditure growth than the current year-by-year gyrations and new gimmicks.

A global budget on national health care, which is only possible when most of the system is under unified financial control, will not only compel attention to cost effectiveness as the only rational and equitable way to ration scarce resources, it will also free physicians from many intrusions into their treatment decisions, as it has done in Canada and Britain. Within the equipment, personnel, and money constraints in a Medicare region, each provider will be free to treat her patients as their medical conditions require. Much less UR of individual patient treatment decisions is necessary (or justified) when impersonal controls over facilities and equipment already set financial limits.

But with Medicare beneficiaries being encouraged into managed care, what about the HMO intrusiveness into medical decisions that produced the backlash of recent years? I think that practice guidelines developed by physician teams rather than by business managers are already beginning to replace arbitrary edicts from management in the better health plans. In addition, new cohorts of physicians will be more accepting of evidence-based guidelines as an aid to good medical practice, rather than seeing them as inappropriate "cookbook" medicine. Another important factor will be the ability to fine-tune the measurement of costs through risk adjustment (i.e., varying a plan's budget in accord with the nature of the patient mix, namely, its age and sickness profile). This fine-tuning is necessary if Medicare payments for HMO enrollees are to provide an appropriate budget within which the individual health plan operates. I admit, however, that as Medicare becomes a series of approaches to health care delivery in the diversified new world of "Medicare + Choice," major adjustments whose design I cannot anticipate will have to be made. But that will be true with or without universalization.

Won't some restrictions on the scope of coverage be needed to adjust Medicare to a global budget? That question brings us to the next element of this scenario: the need for a standard package that will leave out some kinds of treatments for which responsibility will remain private and personal.

A Standard Package

Payers have traditionally accepted the bill for almost any treatment a physician provides, but not quite all. Purely cosmetic surgery is the prototypical exclusion. Many plans have limited mental health care, and some will perhaps eliminate that coverage rather than comply with recent federal legislation mandating parity with physiological needs. The issue of covering Viagra (for male impotence) caused a flap in 1998 and brought to the surface as a question of equity that half of the health plans do not cover any method of contraception. Wanting to limit liability and keep coverage competitive, managed care plans are reviewing other specific coverages. In early 1998, for example, U.S. Healthcare (part of Aetna) eliminated coverage for some advanced fertility treatments—particularly, in vitro fertilization and artificial insemination. In vitro costs $8,000–12,000.

Although some of the insurance industry's warnings that patient rights legislation will necessitate a rise in the price of health insurance are political posturing, they do also contain an element of truth. But there does not have to be an irresolvable dilemma between patients' rights and coverage costs; the coverage variable can be examined more closely, too, and some adjustment of plan scope may well make it feasible to enact needed protective rights without raising premiums.

Several years ago, the AMA's answer to the threat of an expanded government role in health care was its Health Access America proposal, which delineated a standard set of benefits to include acute care, prenatal, well-baby, and diagnostic services. That language is probably too loose to produce any reasonable, easily agreed-upon limitations. The language by which health insurance has tried to define coverage parameters speaks of treatments that are "medically necessary" or "within community standards." Dr. David Eddy has argued that benefits definitions tied to evidence of effectiveness should replace these vague and loose criteria and that doing so is a way to improve the quality of health care.[2]

State Medicaid plans have long defined some conditions that specifically are or are not included, many of them determined by the interest group politicking that lies behind state legislative mandates to insurers. Far and away the boldest and most interesting use of coverage limits, however, is Oregon's use of a priority list of treatments. The list is used to provide the most needed treatments to all those under the poverty income line; in all other state Medicaid programs, a wider spectrum of treatments can only be provided to a portion of the poor. (See Chapter 3.)

In a number of national health systems a model is developing that defines publicly financed "basic" coverage, with supplementary coverage being on a personal or employee-benefit basis. Canada, as mentioned in Chapter 6, is having a federalist dispute over the national requirement of comprehensiveness, as meaning medically necessary. Provinces are challenging the federal guidelines by "delisting" items like annual physicals and reversals of vasectomies. In Britain, severe financial pressures and public dismay over waiting times for nonemergency surgeries have led a number of regional authorities to exclude sex change operations and tattoo removals, as well as cosmetic surgery. One has excluded treatment for 12 conditions, among them varicose veins, wisdom teeth that need to be removed, and snoring! Fertility treatment coverage has large copayments in some regions, and hospitalization for terminal patients also varies widely.

In Germany, 1993 legislation mandated an effort to design a mandatory basic benefits package to replace the comprehensive menu of treatments given in sickness fund rules. Benefits beyond the basic set would be left to voluntary private insurance. Advocates of this narrowing charge that the original ethic of social solidarity, with the healthy helping pay for the sick, has been replaced by a get-what-you-can attitude. They believe personal responsibility needs to be increased and see basic benefits limitations as a way to do the job. This theme may well resonate strongly in the United States. It fits curiously well with another strain of thinking: encouraging patient self-determination and an emphasis on healthier lifestyles to stay well more than acute care to repair body damage. People would have insurance for the bulk of acute care, and employers might (as in Canada and Britain) find it beneficial to employee relations to offer coverage for some excluded conditions (costing far less than current total coverage).

Light at the End of the Health Care Tunnel?

Buffeted first by a false start toward universal coverage in the early 1990s and then by a managed care revolution imposed by private sector actions in the latter part of the decade, Americans may be ready for a breakthrough somewhat earlier than even ardent reformers have dared predict. And it could take a surprisingly familiar form.

Consider the extensions of government-financed health care in recent years. Medicaid coverage has been mandated for low-income pregnant women and children of higher ages—through age 18 by the year 2002. Some of the younger children in families with income up to 133 percent of poverty are now Medicaid eligible. Federal legislation in 1997 authorized a new set of flexible state-designed programs for children not fitting existing categories. These changes are politically and symbolically significant because these children and women do not have to be on welfare to receive health care. And in 1998 President Clinton announced regulatory changes that are expected to add 135,000–200,000 of the working poor to Medicaid. True, Medicaid is means-tested, but acceptance of health insurance assistance is far less demeaning in middle-class eyes than acceptance of welfare as such. And the broader the clientele, the less the perceived indignity.

Within Medicare, note the recently increased scope of screening services authorized in the 1997 Balanced Budget Act: mammography, Pap smears, pelvic exams, colorectal and prostate cancer screening, and bone density measurements. And nary a political stir.

Most recently, the increasing cancellation by employers of health care coverage for under-65 worker retirees has produced proposals, including one by President Clinton, for voluntary Medicare "buy-in" arrangements for some people age 55 to 64.

There is clearly a national willingness to make at least piecemeal extensions of tax-supported health care, and the sky is not falling in. Might it be possible to achieve a broader objective? The answer is, Yes.

A Simple Idea: Universalize Medicare

The way to do it is elegantly simple: Universalize Medicare. The United States should extend Medicare to cover the entire population, gradually expanding it from both the top and the bottom age groups. For example, in the first year cover ages 0–1 and 64. Over some tentatively set period of years (the pace being flexible so as not to add more than some congressionally set percent to the government's financial obligation each year), all Americans could be brought into the same health care tent.

Doesn't this plan mean a large, new federal financial obligation? Yes, directly and immediately. However, the cost would be partly offset at the bottom by gradually eliminating the need for both federal and state Medicaid expenditures. At the upper end, most of the cost would be new for the government but would provide relief for those employers who presently provide coverage for employees under 65. Under-65 adults are healthier on average than those over-65, and providing them health care would therefore cost taxpayers less per person than present Medicare beneficiaries.

Hospital care is the most expensive segment of health care. Would its extension to the currently uninsured mean an exorbitant new cost? No, because it is estimated that the uninsured now receive perhaps 60 percent of the quantity of hospital care received by the well insured. So the increase would be about 40 percent, not 100 percent as some fear. Also, a fourth of the uninsured pool are children, who are low users of hospital care.[3] And the over-65 contingent, who use a lot of care, are already in Medicare.

To achieve any universal coverage system, Americans must learn to think of the nation's health expenditures, private or public, as a single entity. As tax-supported Medicare enlarges, employer and employee private plan premiums and expenses will decline. One might expect businesses and their protective trade associations to welcome being able to cease being the primary responsible party for the nation's health care. Trade unions and employees should be able to achieve some gain in direct wages as their compensation packages are reduced on the benefits side. In other words, the financing of universal Medicare is admittedly a major hurdle to overcome, but the changeover has advantages for all parties, not just the presently uninsured. A major public enlightenment campaign should be able to make the case.

The basic point is that universalizing Medicare would mean a switch in how health care is paid for, not an increase in how much it costs the nation. Less administrative complexity will save money. More fundamentally, nationally gathered and consistently defined clinical data will, in time, make possible a substantial increase in the share of treatment that is evidence-based, which will thus produce more cost effectiveness throughout the system. (See Chapter 8.)

In describing how earlier expansions of tax-supported health care were accomplished, Mary Ruggie asserts that there is "a momentum that tends to occur in social programs when policy statements are properly packaged to reflect prevailing predispositions and institutional arrangements."[4] Medicare has what it takes to support "packaging" that can be both honest and persuasive.

A fact not widely noted is that when Clinton's health plan was being shaped, some legislators and outside policy experts proposed that Medicare be one of the choices in the variety of plans to be offered through the contemplated purchasing "alliances." Because the administration task force was already committed to the concept of managed competition and Medicare was then still a bastion of FFS medicine, the idea was rejected. Jacob S. Hacker suggests that Medicare would have had some good things going for it:

> Medicare, after all, was a highly-developed program with a well-developed institutional infrastructure. Its administrative costs were low [and] it had a system of payment regulation in place. . . . For all its imperfections, Medicare was the largest and most popular federal health program, and the only one whose infrastructure could credibly form the basis of a broader public system.[5]

Because Medicare is now embracing managed care and HMO competition, universalizing it would not undermine current economizing strategies. In fact, having the entire population in a single program could provide the strongest possible push for cost-effective, population-oriented health care. To help things along, Medicare payment provisions could be tweaked, as they already are with some frequency. Indeed, Medicare would be in a position to demand competitive bidding by all the private health plans seeking a piece of the action.

Why not use the payment leverage of the monopsonist federal buyer to encourage large, regional staff/group model, nonprofit HMOs? The nonprofit segment of the American economy is very much alive and well, and in health care specifically there is a long and honorable tradition of nonprofit entities, most notably the thousands of community hospitals that have epitomized the American health care system. And the largest and best known of the HMOs, Kaiser Permanente, is nonprofit. Why not make capital accessible (as the Hill-Burton Act did for hospital construction for many years) to nonprofit health plans, enabling them to expand and compete toe-to-toe with the loosely structured, Wall Street-oriented for-profits?

Although some surveys of nonprofit and for-profit health plans show no conclusive quality difference, some studies of patients with serious and chronic medical problems do indicate better care in nonprofits. A 1997 *U.S. News and World Report* survey using NCQA data on such factors as prevention, physician and member turnover and satisfaction, and access to care found that 33 of 37 top-scoring HMOs were nonprofits.[6] By emphasizing nonprofits in health care, Americans would therefore probably also be emphasizing quality. Health care could then be financed through collective action, employing a mix of tax funding and services provided largely through nonprofit private organizations.

Is this thinking too "far out?" Maybe not as much as it may seem because it does not require a tremendous political fight to eliminate the private sector of providers and health plans, as would adoption of the Canadian system. The private plans could continue, just with a single payer. And this payer, the federal government, would be in a unique position to nudge the private health plans into better health care for all. Furthermore, it leads to major change through incremental steps.

Universal coverage with effective cost controls through global budgeting and fee schedules is a combination that works in most of the Western industrial nations. It can work in the United States, too, and universalizing Medicare is the most rational, least wrenching way to do it. To those who say "Nice, but it's a pipe dream," I would respond with a challenge: What other approach will bring about universal coverage with as little disturbance to the way the U.S. health care delivery system now operates, on a base of more than 30 years of successful operation, and with far lower administrative costs than in the private sector?

Notes

Chapter 1

1. U.S. Census Bureau, "Health Insurance Coverage, 1997" (Washington, D.C.: U.S. Census Bureau, 1998), pp. 60–120.

2. Katherine Levit et al., "National Health Expenditures in 1997: More Slow Growth," *Health Affairs* 17, no. 6 (November/December 1998), pp. 99–110.

3. U.S. Census Bureau, "Health Insurance Coverage, 1997."

4. "Kids at Risk: Uninsured Children Increasingly Come from Middle-Class Families," *U.S. News and World Report* (April 28, 1997).

5. Edwin Chen, "Gap in Health Coverage Hits 'Near-Elderly,'" *Los Angeles Times* (June 1, 1997).

6. Norman Daniels, Donald W. Light, and Ronald L. Caplan, *Benchmarks of Fairness for Health Care Reform* (New York: Oxford University Press, 1996).

7. Larry R. Churchill, *Self-Interest and Universal Health Care* (Cambridge, Mass.: Harvard University Press, 1994), p. 83.

8. Ibid., pp. 29–30.

9. Daniel Callahan, *False Hopes: Why America's Quest for Perfect Health Is a Recipe for Failure* (New York: Simon & Schuster, 1998), pp. 228–232.

10. Ibid., p. 230.

Chapter 2

1. U.S. National Center for Health Statistics, *Vital and Health Statistics*, series 13 (Washington, D.C.: Centers for Disease Control, 1997).

2. Health Insurance Association of America, *Source Book of Health Insurance Data, 1996* (Washington, D.C.: Health Insurance Association of America, 1997), pp. 26–27.

3. Theodore R. Marmor, *The Politics of Medicare* (Chicago: Aldine, 1973), p. 78.

4. U.S. Census Bureau, "Health Insurance Coverage, 1997," (Washington, D.C.: U.S. Census Bureau, 1998), pp. 60–202.

Chapter 3

1. Jacob S. Hacker, *The Road to Nowhere: The Genesis of President Clinton's Plan for Health Security* (Princeton, N.J.: Princeton University Press, 1997), p. 66.

2. Alain C. Enthoven and Richard Kronick, "A Consumer-Choice Health Plan for the 1990s," *New England Journal of Medicine* 320, no. 1 (January 5, 1989), pp. 29–37, and v. 320, no. 2 (January 12, 1989), pp. 94–101. Enthoven's earlier espousal of "regulated

competition" was published in two articles by him in 1978, both under the heading of "A Consumer-Choice Health Plan." Part 1: "Inflation and Inequity in Health Care Today: Alternatives for Cost Control and an Analysis of Proposals for National Health Insurance," *New England Journal of Medicine* 298, no. 12 (March 23, 1978), p. 650–658; Part 2: "A National-Health-Insurance Proposal Based on Regulated Competition in the Private Sector," *New England Journal of Medicine* 298, no. 13 (March 30, 1978), pp. 709–720.

3. Hacker, *The Road to Nowhere*, p. 66.

4. Eugene Declercq and Diana Simmes, "The Politics of 'Drive Through Deliveries': Putting Early Postpartum Discharge on the Legislative Agenda," *Milbank Quarterly* 5, (1997), pp. 175–202.

5. B. Drummond Ayres, Jr., "Political Briefing," *New York Times* (July 24, 1998).

6. Gary Wills, "The War Between the States . . . and Washington," *New York Times Magazine* (July 5, 1998), pp. 26–29.

7. "State Mandated Health Insurance Benefits," excerpted from *State Briefing Book on Health Care* (Washington, D.C.: National Center for Policy Analysis, 1994).

8. Robert Pear, "Hands Tied, Judges Rue Law that Limits H.M.O. Liability," *News York Times* (July 11, 1998).

9. Kathleen S. Andersen, "The Reforming States Group and the Promotion of Federalism," *Milbank Quarterly* 76, no. 1 (Spring 1998), pp. 103–120.

10. Howard M. Leichter, *Health Policy Reform in America: Innovations from the States* (Armonk, N.Y.: M. E. Sharpe, 1997), p. 143, and, generally, pp. 138–162. I have relied heavily on this excellent study of state roles and actions regarding health policy.

11. Ibid., p. 144.

12. Ibid., p. 139.

13. Carol S. Weissert and William G. Weissert, *Governing Health: The Politics of Health Policy* (Baltimore: Johns Hopkins University Press, 1996), p. 53.

14. Haynes Johnson and David S. Broder, *The System: The American Way of Politics at the Breaking Point* (Boston: Little, Brown, 1996), pp. 282–287.

15. Cornelius P. Cotter, *Government and Private Enterprise* (New York: Holt, Rinehart and Winston, 1960), p. 450.

16. Note in *Los Angeles Times* (June 24, 1998).

17. Wayne J. Guglielmo, "Organized Medicine—Dying or Just Fading Away?" *Medical Economics (General Surgery)* (April 1998), pp. 26–40.

18. John D. Cochrane, "Year of the Consumer," *Integrated Healthcare Report* (March 1997), pp. 1–12.

19. Johnson and Broder, *The System*, pp. 630–631.

20. Gina Kolata, "How Demand Surged for Unapproved Prostate Test," *New York Times* (September 29, 1993).

21. Ibid.

22. Scott Stern et al., "Detection of Prostate and Colon Cancer," *JAMA* 280, no. 2 (July 8, 1998), pp. 117–118.

23. On the politics of abortion, see Karen O'Connor, *No Neutral Ground: Abortion Politics in an Age of Absolutes* (Boulder, Colo.: Westview Press, 1996).

24. Mary Lee Seifert, Stephen K. Heffler, and Carolyn S. Donham, "Hospital, Employment, and Price Indicators for the Health Care Industry: Third Quarter, 1997," *Health Care Financing Review* 19, no. 3 (Spring 1998), pp. 105–149.

25. Mark A. Rodman, "Consumer Protection and Managed Care: The Need for Organized Consumers," *Health Affairs* 15, no. 3 (Fall 1996), pp. 110–123.

Chapter 4

1. Sherry Glied, *Chronic Condition: Why Health Reform Fails* (Cambridge: Harvard University Press, 1977), pp. 92–93.

2. "NCQA Releases First Annual *State of Managed Care Quality* Report" (October 1, 1997) at www.ncqa.org.

3. Arnold M. Epstein, "Rolling Down the Runway: The Challenges Ahead for Quality Report Cards," *Journal of the American Medical Association* 279, no. 21 (June 3, 1998), pp. 1691–1696.

4. Epstein, "Rolling Down the Runway," pp. 1691–1696.

5. Robert A. Rosenblatt, "Gore Advocates Health Plan Standards," *Los Angeles Times* (June 18, 1998).

6. Donald M. Berwick, "The Total Customer Relationship in Health Care," *Journal on Quality Improvement* 23, no. 5 (May 1997), pp. 245–250.

7. Robert J. Blendon et al., "Understanding the Managed Care Backlash," *Health Affairs* 17, no. 4 (July/Aug 1998), pp. 80–94.

8. K. Lohr, *Medicare: A Strategy for Quality Assurance* (Washington, D.C.: National Academy Press, 1990), p. 441.

9. Mark A. Schuster et al., *Why the Quality of U.S. Health Care Must Be Improved* (Santa Monica, Cal.: RAND, October 1997), p. 1.

10. Peter T. Kilborn, "Poor Workers Turning Down Employers' Health Benefits," *New York Times* (November 10, 1997).

11. AARP Public Policy Institute, *Coming Up Short: Increasing Out-of-Pocket Health Spending by Older Americans,* rev. ed. (Washington, D.C.: AARP Public Policy Institute, April 1995), p. 11.

12. AARP Public Policy Institute, *Out-of-Pocket Health Spending by Medicare Beneficiaries Age 65 and Older: 1997 Projections* (Washington, D.C.: AARP Public Policy Institute, December 1997), p. 17.

13. Marc L. Berk and Alan C. Monheit, "The Concentration of Health Expenditures: An Update," *Health Affairs* 11, no. 4 (Winter 1992), pp. 145–149.

14. Mary A. Laschober and Gary L. Olin, *Health and Health Care of the Medicare Population* (Rockville, Md.: Westat, 1996), p. 27.

15. Katherine Levit et al., "National Health Expenditures in 1997: More Slow Growth," *Health Affairs* 17, no. 6 (November/December 1998), pp. 99–110.

16. Congressional Budget Office, *Projections of National Health Expenditures, 1997–2008* (Washington, D.C.: Congressional Budget Office, 1998).

17. Robert A. Rosenblatt, "Number of Americans Lacking Health Insurance on Rise," *Los Angeles Times* (September 11, 1996).

18. David W. Liska, *The Uninsured in the United States* (Washington, D.C.: Urban Institute, 1996).

19. Paul B. Ginsburg and Jeremy D. Pickreigh, "Tracking Health Care Costs," *Health Affairs* 16, no. 4 (July/August 1997).

20. Jon R. Gabel, Paul B. Ginsburg, and Kelly Hunt, "Small Employers and Their Health Benefits, 1988–1996: An Awkward Adolescence, *Health Affairs* 16, no. 5 (September/October 1997), pp. 103–110.

21. U.S. Census Bureau, "Health Insurance Coverage, 1997" (Washington, D.C.: U.S. Census Bureau, 1998), p. 60–202.

22. General Accounting Office, *Employment-Based Health Insurance: Costs Increase and Family Coverage Decreases,* Report HEHS-97-35 (February 24, 1997).

23. Peter P. Budetti, "Health Insurance for Children—A Model for Incremental Health Reform?" *New England Journal of Medicine* 338, no. 8 (February 19, 1998), pp. 541–542.

24. Thomas M. Selden, Jessica S. Banthin, and Joel W. Cohen, "Medicaid's Problem Children: Eligible but Not Enrolled," *Health Affairs* 17, no. 3 (May/June 1998), pp. 192–200.

25. Steven A. Schroeder, "The Medically Uninsured: Will They Always Be with Us?" *New England Journal of Medicine* 334, no. 17 (April 25, 1996), pp. 1130–1133.

26. Edwin Chen, "Number Without Health Insurance Rises," *Los Angeles Times* (April 27, 1996).

27. Paul W. Newacheck et al., "Health Insurance and Access to Primary Care for Children," *New England Journal of Medicine* 338, no. 8 (February 19, 1998), pp. 513–518.

28. See Charles F. Andrain, *Public Health Policies and Social Inequality* (London: Macmillan, 1998).

29. Thomas A. Preston, *The Clay Pedestal,* 2d ed., (New York: Scribner's, 1986), p. 147.

Chapter 5

1. U.S. Census Bureau, quoted in Marilyn Moon, *Medicare Now and in the Future,* 2nd ed. (Washington, D.C.: Urban Institute Press, 1996), p. 7.

2. AARP, *A Profile of Older Americans, 1997* (Washington, D.C.: AARP, 1997).

3. Daniel Callahan's figures, quoted in Melvin Konner, *Medicine at the Crossroads: The Crisis in Health Care* (New York: Vintage, 1994), p. 177.

4. George Rosen, quoted in Konner, *Medicine at the Crossroads,* p. 55.

5. Congressional Budget Office, *Revised Baseline Budget Projections for Fiscal Years 1999–2008* (Washington, D.C.: Congressional Budget Office, March 3, 1998).

6. AARP and Administration on Aging, *A Profile of Older Americans: 1997* (Washington, D.C.: AARP and Administration on Aging, 1997).

7. Robert O Morgan et al., "The Medicare-HMO Revolving Door—The Healthy Go in and the Sick Go Out," *New England Journal of Medicine* 337, no. 3 (July 17, 1997), pp. 169–175.

8. Robert Pear, "Policy Changes Fail to Fill Gaps in Health Coverage," *New York Times* (August 9, 1998).

9. *AARP Bulletin* (May 1995).

Chapter 6

1. *New State Ice Co.* v. *Leibman,* 285 U.S. 262 (1932). (With thanks to Professor Joseph R. Reisert for locating this elusive reference).

2. See Gwendolyn Gray, *Federalism and Health Policy* (Toronto: University of Toronto Press, 1991).

3. Personal communication, Geoffrey Ballinger, Canadian Institute of Health Information, August 28, 1998.

4. Morris L. Barrer et al., "Re-minding Our Ps and Qs: Medical Cost Controls in Canada," *Health Affairs* 15, no. 2 (Summer 1996), pp. 216–234.

5. Canadian Institute of Health Information, *1997 Health Expenditures,* at www.cihi.ca.

6. From provincial health plan descriptions found at the Health Canada website: www.hc=sc/gc/ca/english.

7. Speaking notes of Alan Nymark, Associate Deputy Health Minister, addressing Pulse '98 in Toronto, Ontario, May 11, 1998.

8. "Waiting for Dobbo," *Economist* (May 23, 1998).

9. "Bevan's Baby Hits Middle Age," *Economist* (July 4, 1998).

10. Robert G. Evans, quoted in John K. Iglehart, "Canada's Health Care System Faces Its Problems," *New England Journal of Medicine* 322, no. 8 (February 22, 1990), pp. 562–568.

11. "Waiting for Dobbo."

12. Rudolf Klein, "Why Britain Is Reorganizing Its National Health Service—Yet Again," *Health Affairs* 17, no. 4 (July/August 1998), pp. 111–125.

13. Quoted in Sarah Lyall, "For British Health System, Bleak Prognosis," *New York Times* (January 30, 1997).

14. *Statement by the Chancellor of the Exchequer on the Comprehensive Spending Review—14 July 1998.* (www.hm-treasury.gov.uk).

15. Peter Knuth et al., "The German Health System: Lessons for Reform in the United States," *Archives of Internal Medicine* 15 (August 11–25, 1997), p. 73.

16. "Downhill Slide, Uphill Struggler: Paying for a Mountain of Health-Care Bills," *Economist* 338, no. 7950 (January 27, 1996), p. 11.

17. H. K. Selbmann et al., "Country Profile—Germany," *Lancet* 348, no. 9042 (December 14, 1996), pp. 1631–1639.

18. Uwe Reinhardt, "Germany's Health Care System: It's Not the American Way," *Health Affairs* 13, no. 4 (Fall, 1994), pp. 22–24.

Chapter 7

1. Kaiser/Harvard, "Is There a Managed Care 'Backlash'?" Press Release (November 5, 1997) at www.kff.org.

2. UCBerkeley/Field Research survey, reported in David R. Olmos, "State Survey Finds 42 Percent Had Problems in Managed Care," *Los Angeles Times* (December 4, 1997), p. A1.

3. "How Americans Perceive the Health Care System," survey by International Communications Research for National Coalition on Health Care (January 1997), at www.americashealth.org.

4. Robert J. Blendon et al., "Understanding the Managed Care Backlash," *Health Affairs* 17, no. 4 (July/Aug 1998), pp. 80–94.

5. Ivana Krajcinovic, *From Company Doctors to Managed Care: The United Mineworkers' Noble Experiment* (Ithaca, N.Y.: Cornell University Press, 1997).

6. Michael L. Millenson, *Demanding Medical Excellence* (Chicago: University of Chicago Press, 1997), pp. 167–168.

7. Robert Kuttner, "Must Good HMOs Go Bad?" *New England Journal of Medicine* 338, no. 21 (May 21, 1998), pp. 1558–1563.

8. Press Release, Interstudy Publications Industry Report, November 12, 1998, at www.hmodata.com.

9. Interstudy Publications HMO Directory 7.2, 1997, at www.hmodata.com.

10. *New York Times* (November 24, 1997).

11. Millenson, *Demanding Medical Excellence*, pp. 216–222.

12. See articles in *Health Affairs* 16, no. 6 (November–December 1997) pp. 115–141.

13. Eli Ginzberg, *Tomorrow's Hospital* (New Haven: Yale University Press, 1996), p. 43.

14. National Center for Health Statistics, *National Hospital Discharge Survey, 1995,* Series 13, No. 133 (January 1988), in *Statistical Abstracts of the United States, 1996.*

Chapter 8

1. Sheila Smith et al., "The Next Ten Years of Health Spending: What Does the Future Hold?" *Health Affairs* 17, no. 5 (September/October 1998), pp. 128–140.

2. William B. Schwartz, *Life Without Disease: The Pursuit of Medical Utopia* (Berkeley: University of California Press, 1998), p. 27.

3. Abigail Zuger, "Do Breast Self-Exams Save Lives? Science Still Doesn't Have Answer," *New York Times* (January 6, 1998).

4. John E. Wennberg, "Dealing with Medical Practice Variations," *Health Affairs* 3, no. 2 (Summer 1994), pp. 6–32.

5. Center for the Evaluative Clinical Sciences, Dartmouth Medical School, *The Dartmouth Atlas of Health Care 1998* (New York: Oxford University Press, 1998).

6. Robert A. Rosenblatt, "Putting Surgery on the Map," *Los Angeles Times* (October 20, 1997).

7. Ibid.

8. John E. Wennberg, "The Paradox of Appropriate Care," *Journal of the American Medical Association* 258, no. 18 (November 13, 1987), pp. 2568–2569.

9. David M. Eddy, "Variations in Physician Practice: The Role of Uncertainty," *Health Affairs* 3, no. 2 (Summer 1984), pp. 74–80.

10. "Practice Guidelines," *Medical Management Network* 5 no. 9 (October 1997), pp. 1–3.

11. Jeffrey S. Rose, *Medicine and the Information Age* (Tampa, Fla.: American College of Physician Executives, 1998), p. 233.

12. John E. Wennberg, "The Paradox of Appropriate Care," *Journal of the American Medical Association* 258, no. 18 (November 13, 1987), pp. 2568–2569.

13. Neil A. Lewis, "Agency Facing Revolt After Report," *New York Times* (September 14, 1995).

14. Susan Gilbert, "No Benefit Found for Fetal Monitors," *New York Times* (January 13, 1998).

15. "Keeping Patients Warm Prevents Heart Attacks," *Health* (January/February 1998), p. 73.

16. David M. Eddy, "Health System Reform: Will Controlling Costs Require Rationing Services?" *Journal of the American Medical Association* 272, no. 4 (July 27, 1994), pp. 324–328.

17. David M. Eddy, "Rationing Resources While Improving Quality: How to Get More for Less," *Journal of the American Medical Association* 272, no. 10 (September 14, 1994), pp. 817–824.

18. Eddy, "Rationing Resources," p. 820.

19. Philip F. Cooper and Barbara Steinberg Schone, "More Offers, Fewer Takers for Employment-Based Health Insurance, 1987 and 1996," *Health Affairs* 16, no. 6 (November/December 1997), pp. 142–149.

20. Lynn Payer, *Medicine and Culture: Varieties of Treatment in the United States, England, West Germany, and France* (New York: Henry Holt, 1988), p. 127.

21. Henry J. Aaron and William B. Schwartz, *The Painful Prescription: Rationing Hospital Care* (Washington, D.C.: The Brookings Institution, 1984).

Chapter 9

1. Pat Armstrong and Hugh Armstrong, with Claudia Fegan, *Universal Health Care: What the United States Can Learn from the Canadian Experience* (New York: New Press, 1998), p. 74.

2. David M. Eddy, "Benefit Language," *Journal of the American Medical Association* 275, no. 8 (February 28, 1996), pp. 650–658.

3. Eli Ginzberg, *Tomorrow's Hospital* (New Haven: Yale University Press, 1996), p. 122.

4. Mary Ruggie, *Realignments in the Welfare State: Health Policy in the United States, Britain, and Canada* (New York: Columbia University Press, 1996), p. 140.

5. Jacob S. Hacker, *The Road to Nowhere: The Genesis of President Clinton's Plan for Health Security* (Princeton, N.J.: Princeton University Press, 1997), p. 128.

6. Cited in Robert Kuttner, "Must Good HMOs Go Bad?" *New England Journal of Medicine* 338, no. 21 (May 21, 1998), pp. 1558–1563. See also David M. Lawrence et al., "Trusting in the Future: The Distinct Advantage of Nonprofit HMOs," *Milbank Quarterly* 75, no. 1 (1997), pp. 5–10.

Index

Abortion, 54–55
Accreditation, 136
Advance directives. *See* Living wills
Advantages of managed care, 116–119
Advisory Commission on Consumer
    Protection and Quality in the Health
    Care Industry, 39, 115
Advisory Council of the Ministry of Health, 105
Agency for Health Care Policy and Research
    (AHCPR), 47, 61, 118, 133–134, 137
Aid to Families with Dependent Children
    (AFDC), 86
Alzheimers Association, 49
Amenities of care, 145, 154
American Association of Health Plans
    (AAHP), 110, 124
American Association of Retired Persons
    (AARP), 52, 155
American Cancer Society, 52, 132
American College of Nursing Midwives, 37
American College of Physicians, 52, 67–68
American Dental Association, 52
American Diabetes Association, 48
American Health Care Association, 50
American Heart Association, 48–49
American Hospital Association (AHA), 20, 49,
    66
American Legion, 47
American Medical Association (AMA), 25, 49,
    78, 156–157
American Medical Political Action Committee
    (AMPAC), 52
American Nurses Association, 50, 63
American Urological Society, 52
Angioplasties, 132
Antibiotics, 143
Armed forces. *See* Military health services
Armey, Dick, 116

Balance billing, 93
Balanced Budget Act (BBA), 29, 38, 65, 75, 80,
    158

Benchmarks of Fairness for Health Care Reform
    (Daniels), 14
Benefits. *See* Standard benefits
Beveridge Report, 99
Birth procedures, 5, 21, 132, 136, 137, 146
Bismarck, Chancellor, 20, 103
Blair, Tony, 100–101
Blue Cross, 20, 21, 50
Blue Shield, 20, 50, 52
Boston, 133
Brandeis, Louis, 92
Breast cancer research, 132, 140
Britain. *See* United Kingdom
British Medical Association, 99
British North America Act, 92
Broder, David S., 51
Budgets. *See* Costs
Bush, George, 35, 134

California, 7, 24, 113, 116, 124, 133, 137,
    144–145
Callahan, Daniel, 16
Canada, 69, 91–96, 97–98, 153–154, 157
Canada Health Act, 94, 96
Canadian Medical Association (CMA), 93, 95
Capitalism, 3–4
Capitation, 21, 22, 29, 110, 113, 130
Catholic Health Association, 49
CAT scans, 135
Centers for Disease Control (CDC), 4, 47
Cesarean birth procedures, 132, 136
Charitable foundations, 49
"Cherry picking," 120
Chicago Hope, 19
Children, 10. *See also* Medicaid
    and employer-paid health care, 7–8, 67–68
Children's Health Insurance Program, 38
Churchill, Larry R., 15–16
Clinton, Bill, 5, 13, 29, 115–116, 149, 158
    Health Security Plan, 5, 28, 33–40, 46, 50,
    149, 152–153, 160
Clinton, Hilary Rodham, 35